D1188765

TAKE HEART
Expand your vision of God

For Leo & Margaret

Best wishes

Tim C.Ss.R

Timothy J. Buckley C.Ss.R.

A Redemptorist Publication

Published by **Redemptorist Publications**
A Registered Charity limited by guarantee. Registered in England 3261721.

Copyright © Timothy J. Buckley C.Ss.R., 2009

First published June 2009

Layout: Peena Lad
Cover design: Chris Nutbeen

ISBN 978-0-85231-355-8

All scripture quotations are from THE JERUSALEM BIBLE, © 1966 by Darton, Longman & Todd, Ltd. and Doubleday, a division of Random House, Inc. reprinted by permission. Psalms from *The Psalms: A New Translation* © 1963 The Grail (England) published by HarperCollins. Used with permission.

A CIP catalogue record for this book is available from the British Library.

Printed by Joseph Ball Printers Limited

Redemptorist

P U B L I C A T I O N S
Alphonsus House Chawton Hampshire GU34 3HQ
Telephone 01420 88222 Fax 01420 88805
rp@rpbooks.co.uk   www.rpbooks.co.uk

Contents

Acknowledgements

I am indebted to many people for this publication, and I hope the material in the book itself expresses my gratitude to all of you who have been part of my life to date. I am especially grateful to my confrères Frank Dickinson, Kevin Callaghan and Tony Hodgetts, for reading the early drafts and for their wise and helpful comments. Sadly Tony died on 14th September 2008: may he rest in peace. I am grateful to Peter Edwards for his meticulous work as copy-editor, which also included many helpful suggestions, and to Denis McBride, Andrew Lyon and the whole team at Redemptorist Publications for keeping faith in the project. To all of you, I say, "take heart".

Timothy Buckley is a priest in the Redemptorist Congregation. Born in 1946, he joined the Redemptorists in 1964. Ordained in 1970, he spent much of that decade giving missions and retreats and as vocations director. In the 1980s he served as a parish priest in Birmingham and Sunderland, and during the 1990s he was engaged in the formation and training of students preparing for ministry. He gained an MA in Christian Spirituality from Creighton University, Omaha, USA, and has a doctorate from Heythrop College, London University. His thesis on the pastoral care of Catholics who experience marital breakdown was published in 1997 under the title *What Binds Marriage? Roman Catholic Theology in Practice.* A second edition was published by Continuum in 2002. He was Publishing Director of Redemptorist Publications for six years from the beginning of 2001 and has now returned to giving missions and retreats.

A word to the reader

Every so often we meet people who have a marked influence on our lives. I will always be indebted to Marty Palmer, a Jesuit scripture scholar, whose foundation course during a Spirituality Summer School at Creighton University in Omaha, Nebraska, in 1989 made an enormous impression on me. He transformed my understanding of the scriptures and therefore my view of the world and my preaching ministry. Sadly I learnt that Marty died an untimely death in his late fifties. I pray that now he may be enjoying the fruits of the redemption and the vision of the Lord that he so eloquently expounded to his students.

Introducing his subject, Marty Palmer distributed a sheet of paper, naming the twenty-seven books of the New Testament, and beside each book were two blank boxes. He advised us that an essential element of the course was that we read the whole of the New Testament twice, ticking off the books as we completed them. The books could be read in any order and he was not expecting us to dwell on the message or meditate on particular passages but just to get the overall picture and as far as possible note the connections. I recommend this exercise, at least the reading of each book once. You will not be disappointed. You will read passages that are never read in the liturgical cycles and you will probably be surprised at the connections you will make.

Initially I would like to suggest that you also approach the reading of this book as a text to be read through rather than meditated upon. I would be flattered if afterwards you felt drawn to return to certain sections for further reflection but, drawing on my own experience, I have tried to write freely and present an overall vision, looking for connections as the story unfolds. It is very much the way I have approached my preaching ministry on missions and retreats over many years. As I hope will become obvious by the end, it is the oneness of the message, powerfully expressed in the unity and integrity of the scriptures, which I am seeking to present. Accordingly I have tried to write in an uncomplicated style. For the most part I have used the *Jerusalem Bible* translation and the Grail translation of the Psalms because these are the ones that will be familiar to Catholics from the liturgy. I have offered scripture references and acknowledged my sources, but I have also tried to keep footnotes and references to a minimum.

This may all come as a surprise to those who are familiar with my only other major publication, *What Binds Marriage? Roman Catholic Theology in Practice*.[1] I remember a feeling of embarrassment when a good friend of mine, who had taught English all her life, noted that she needed a dictionary by her side when reading it. In my defence, it was an edited version of my doctoral thesis, and the history of the Church's understanding of marriage is not exactly simple. However, I did try to present the results of my research into the Church's pastoral response to marriage breakdown as coherently and as simply as possible. It was very rewarding to have been able to undertake the work for the Bishops' Conference of England and Wales in the early 1990s and in the first instance to present the bishops with a report in 1994. At the heart of my findings was the utter conviction that no matter how much a person's life may have disintegrated, there can be no one and no group of people considered beyond the redeeming power of Christ's love. To that extent I see this volume as a sequel to my work on marriage breakdown, and I am confident that this time my friend will not need a dictionary by her side.

As a Catholic priest, naturally my Christian experience has been shaped by the Catholic tradition, but I hope it will be quickly obvious that I am totally committed to the work of ecumenism. Therefore I hope that what I have written will put fresh heart into Christians from other traditions too and I sincerely hope that I have not expressed anything in a way that may appear insensitive to them.

---

1 London: Continuum, 2002.

Chapter One
Starting afresh

Take heart

In the Acts of the Apostles we are told that Paul and Barnabas "went back through Lystra and Iconium to Antioch. They put fresh heart into the disciples, encouraging them to persevere in the faith" (14:21-22). It was these words that inspired me to entitle this book *Take Heart: Expand your Vision of God*. I am a member of the Redemptorist Congregation and for long periods in my life I have been an itinerant preacher. I can think of no better rallying call for the Redemptorist of today than to go from place to place putting "fresh heart into the disciples".

Certainly in Western Christendom we face major challenges and I do not think it is an exaggeration to say that many people are becoming disheartened. In the Catholic Church the scandal of children being abused by clerics has had enormous repercussions and we face the continuing effects of the decline in vocations to the priesthood and religious life, which is forcing us to think again about the nature of priesthood and ministry. In general young people are not as committed to churchgoing as their parents and grandparents. In Britain today the secular agenda is squeezing religion to the margins and there is a real concern that our Christian heritage is being lost. But that is not the whole story. The Church has lived through far more difficult times and survived different kinds of persecution throughout its history. At the heart of the Gospel is a message that stands the test of time and is relevant in every age and in every corner of the world. It is that which gives me heart and which I trust will inspire the reader also to live in the hope of seeing the promises of Jesus fulfilled.

I want to begin by reaffirming the faith of my childhood and the faith in which I have ministered as a priest for over thirty-eight years of my life. At the same time I am conscious that my understanding of the faith has evolved in such a way that many of my childhood perceptions and even those of later years have been superseded by what I trust is a more balanced and mature understanding and a more expansive vision of God.

Motivation and recognition

St Paul acknowledges that when he was a child he used "to talk like a child, and think like a child, and argue like a child" (1 Corinthians 13:11), but insists that when he grew up he put childish ways behind him. The secret of healthy living is that we mature at every level of our nature and being, but that is easier said than done. As modern psychologists love to remind us, we all carry a lot of baggage from the past and much of it may be subconscious. Unless and until we learn to deal with some of this baggage our growth may well be stunted and our ability to live life to the full, which is what Jesus invites us to do (John 10:10), is limited. I hope it becomes apparent in this book that I am convinced that another of Paul's insights is true: namely that God can turn everything to good for those who love him (Romans 8:28). The most wonderful thing for us as Christians is that we do not have to live our lives full of regrets. When we expose everything, including our weaknesses, disappointments and failures, to the light of Christ, then our eyes are opened and we are given a new perspective, which gives meaning to the whole of our lives.

From the very beginning human beings have sought to understand themselves and the world in which they live. We seek meaning and purpose and need a reason to get up in the morning. We need motivation to get on with the business of living and the assurance that what we do and who we are is leading to some kind of fulfilment. The mystery of death is the ultimate challenge and I find it fascinating that even someone as avowedly atheistic as Richard Dawkins cannot help but reveal an instinctive desire to fashion some meaning or at least seek some consolation in the face of this ultimate reality. In his preface to the paperback edition of his book *The God Delusion*, he introduces us to David Ashton, whose son, Luke, had sadly died an untimely death at the age of seventeen.[1] Dawkins wants us to know that what was significant about this death for him was that, as a memorial to Luke, over £2,000 was collected at the funeral for Dawkins' charitable foundation, established to encourage reason and science. Understandably he was touched by the fact that they appreciated his work and that the funeral service included the opening lines of his book *Unweaving the Rainbow*, a text that he has also earmarked for his own funeral.

---

1 R. Dawkins, *The God Delusion* (London: Black Swan, 2007), p. 21.

As I read Dawkins' account of these events I was reminded of the many funerals I have celebrated and how much it meant to me to know that the families and friends of the people who had died had been consoled by the experience. But were we all deluding ourselves into believing that this was not the end – that those who had died had been called to a new and better life with God? I am not ashamed to admit that over the years I have wondered and had my doubts. I find it consoling to realise that I am not alone. When Cardinal Basil Hume was suddenly faced with the reality of his incurable cancer he admitted that he wrestled with the ultimate questions that confront us all. Monsignor George Stack quoted the Cardinal at the Requiem Mass in Westminster Cathedral on the evening he died:

> First thoughts about death are normally ones of fear and dread. It is partly having to face the unknown, partly recoiling from the final agony as we lie helpless and perhaps wired up to all those machines competing for access to our body. Some thoughts tell us there is no future, only a blank nothing, we are no more. Another thought comes and tells us how quickly we are forgotten. In a very bad moment, I think about the relief my death will bring to some people. I worry about the insensitive and clumsy ways I have handled some people.
>
> But there is another voice that speaks within us. It is not a voice that depresses and frightens. It has a different message. You have loved so many people in your life; are you to be frustrated and denied that love which you have sought throughout your life? It is not so.
>
> This is an instinct which speaks of hope leading to life after death… That instinct beckons us… Then faith finally takes over and triumphantly declares "It is so." The instinct for survival is a true one. It does not deceive. How could it be otherwise since it is God-given? Faith brings the reassurance which instinct was seeking.[2]

Faith

So what is this faith? Firstly it is not belief in religion or a religious system, or belief in a set of doctrines or even a creed. The faith that Cardinal Hume speaks of and the faith about which I will write in this

---

2 *Homilies Given at the Funeral Rites of Cardinal George Basil Hume, OSB, OM* (London: Westminster Cathedral, 1999), pp. 9-10.

book is faith in a person, the person of Jesus of Nazareth. When I try to make this point with children I tell them a story about Freddie Freckles. Freddie is lost and looks around for someone to give him directions. He sees a policeman nearby and approaches him. He has been taught that the policeman is someone he can trust! He follows the policeman's directions and all is well. The point we try to draw out is that Freddie does not make an act of faith in the directions but in the policeman. When I say I believe, I am making an act of faith in a person whom I can trust. I can say that I believe in Jesus of Nazareth because his guidance and his teaching have been revelations to me. Jesus has shown me how to understand and interpret my experience of life and of death. In the face of all the challenges and the confusions, the disappointments and the uncertainty, I still wish to renew that faith and suggest that in doing so I am making a very rational judgement.

My faith is not unquestioning: quite the opposite. As I hope will become apparent, one of the great discoveries in my life has been the realisation that I am free, that the Lord came to set me free, and that it is all right to admit that I have my doubts and that I do not have all the answers. I am convinced that the faith I and so many others live and celebrate is not irrational but is the fruit of years of prayer and reflection on our experience. When you pick up any of the books of scripture, you are reading how those who have gone before us have sought to make sense of their experiences just as we do of ours. Of course, if you do not grasp this fact, understanding the God of the Old Testament in particular becomes a very hazardous business. Today we are blessed to have the work of scripture scholars and theologians who help us to interpret these ancient and inspirational texts. Later in this book we will have a look at the meaning of inspiration, but for now it is enough to note that we do not believe that God dictated the biblical texts verbatim. They were written by ordinary people living within the limits of their own understanding and experience but inspired, we believe, to reveal God's presence and purposes. The age-old battle between science and religion will probably continue until the end of time, but I find it baffling that even today there are those who take a fundamentalist stand and insist that the only valid interpretation of scripture is a literal one; and baffling that creationism attracts so many adherents.[3] It never ceases to

---

3 While creationism covers a wide range of beliefs I am using it here of those Christians who insist on the literal interpretation of the creation texts in Genesis.

10

fascinate me that people who show themselves to be highly intelligent in every other aspect of their lives suddenly become trapped in an almost infantile cocoon when it comes to religion.

Reverence for the mystery and miracles

The religious dialogue with science calls for mature people listening to one another and rejoicing in the discoveries that open up the mystery of our universe to us. By way of example I will never forget a groundbreaking documentary, made in 1983, which for the first time filmed the process of human conception. The BBC edited what was originally a Swedish film and presented it in its *Horizon* series. The drama that unfolds in human intercourse was examined in detail and the moment filmed when, after one of the 300 million-plus spermatozoa ejaculated by the male has made the journey to the woman's ovum in the Fallopian tube, it finally penetrates and fertilises that ovum. We are reminded that both the ovum and the sperm contain twenty-three chromosomes, which make up the forty-six chromosomes that will determine the unique DNA in every cell of that human body. The first cell divides and continues to divide until the six million cells that make up the body are formed. We also view the development of the embryo into a foetus and the growth of the baby in the womb until finally it is born.

This programme was not a religious programme, yet it was presented almost reverentially, inviting us to marvel at the wonder of it all. For example, just prior to the moment of fertilisation we were told that "one of those fascinating and hard-to-explain biological phenomena occurs". It was the fact that the ovum rolls like a planet in space and always counterclockwise. We were also told of other developments that cannot be explained, like the plugs that form in the nose of the unborn child. And the title of the programme was *The Miracle of Life*.

Many people have real problems with miracles, which they see defined simply as the suspending of the laws of nature by the intervention of God. I admit that these are delicate areas and there is always a danger that religious people may move into the realm of superstition, but I would suggest that there remains much that is a mystery to us and that will always remain a mystery to us, no matter how many scientific breakthroughs are made. It is when we view ourselves and the universe with a sense of awe and wonder that I believe we touch the miraculous and are open to the mystery of God's providential presence. It is then that we learn to be humble, a prerequisite for the spiritual life and for relationship with God.

We will see when we unravel the Genesis story of creation that the real temptation for our first parents was not to steal a piece of forbidden fruit but to believe that they could control the world. It is a temptation that has lost none of its strength today and I believe the biblical stories are as relevant to our own times as they were when the authors recorded them.

The yearning for fulfilment

You do not need to be a trained psychologist to recognise in yourself and in all human beings an innate desire for personal fulfilment. We all want to know that we are valued and loved. The baby craves attention and will not be silenced until its appetites both for food and affection are satisfied. And, one way or another, these cravings go on throughout our lives. Sadly many people do not mature into rounded, well-balanced adults and they spend their lives demanding attention in ways that can be destructive both for themselves and those around them. For example, in today's world fame has become a criterion for success and acceptance, yet paradoxically it can also be a powerfully destructive force, undermining people's reputations and confidence as quickly as it has built them up. And it is precisely because of the fact that life is so full of these paradoxes that to live well-balanced and fulfilled lives will always be an enormous challenge. How do we harness the energy that equips us to strive for success and at the same time cope with the disappointment when our ambitions are thwarted? As someone once wryly remarked to me: "Even Mother Teresa of Calcutta had to get her kicks from something!" What you and I and Mother Teresa wish to know is that at the end of each day we can rest secure in the knowledge that something was achieved – ideally the best we could muster. Sadly such satisfaction is often not easy to come by. Most of us have to deal with our neuroses and it would seem that deep down many of us struggle with poor self-images, not sure of our worth or whether we really are lovable.

However, when I read the Gospel, Jesus does offer me marvellous insights into who I am and where I fit in. In the first place it becomes clear that I am acceptable to and loved by him and his Father and that not only do I not have to earn their love and acceptance, but it is actually impossible for me to do so. The real paradox is that only in so far as I am willing to let go and abandon myself to God can I become my real self. It is then that, free from the preoccupation of trying to convince myself and others that I am lovable, I can get on with the business of living. But, make no mistake, this is a lifetime's work and does not come easily.

So the search for fulfilment would seem to be a human instinct. Judged by this criterion even our unsocial or unacceptable behaviour can be explained. The young tearaway who makes everyone's life a misery is probably desperate to be noticed, maybe to compensate for the affirmation he failed to receive in his earlier formative years. Please do not imagine that here I am trying to excuse all crime and bad behaviour or seeking excuses for all our failures. I simply wish to highlight the fundamental motivating force in all our lives. So, if it is true that we need a reason to get up in the morning, it is equally true that deep down we desire to retire in the evening at peace with ourselves and the world. As the psalmist so beautifully expresses it:

> I will lie down in peace and sleep comes at once
> for you alone, Lord, make me dwell in safety. (Psalm 4:9)

The moral struggle

Of course, no matter how hard we try, we do not go to bed every night satisfied and at peace. Apart from all the outside forces that disturb us, we also have ourselves to contend with. St Paul describes these struggles in language with which I anticipate most of us can identify:

> I cannot understand my own behaviour. I fail to carry out the things I want to do, and I find myself doing the very things I hate… for though the will to do what is good is in me, the performance is not, with the result that instead of doing the good things I want to do, I carry out the sinful things I do not want. (Romans 7:15. 18-19)

Paul is analysing the nature of sin within him and of course points to the solution when a few verses later he cries out: "What a wretched man I am! Who will rescue me from this body doomed to death? Thanks be to God through Jesus Christ our Lord!" (7:24-25).

There is an argument prevalent today that morality does not need an outside agent like God to provide the moral imperatives by which we live. It suggests that, as in every other sphere of life, human beings are evolving and reaching accepted and acceptable codes of behaviour. Indeed, in spite of all the problems facing the world, it concludes that the consensus moves inexorably towards higher moral standards, and cites the widespread outlawing of all forms of discrimination and the growing abandonment of the death penalty as indicators. The problem with this approach is that it is based on the belief that just as natural selection explains how everything has evolved to date, so everything is inevitably working to some kind of natural fulfilment. The problem with this is that it cannot find room for personal failure. For me Paul's words ring true and I am convinced that my struggles are not purely the result of a Catholic guilt instilled in me from childhood. It is interesting that groups like Alcoholics Anonymous, which follow the twelve-step programme, insist that progress is impossible unless those with addictions accept dependence on God. With those who profess to be atheists or agnostics they simply ask them to put aside all prejudice and all preconceived notions of God and at least accept a spiritual power upon which they can depend and that can effect change, and I think their success rate in this field of human tragedy is not to be underestimated. The other Christian parallel with the twelve-step programme is the need for communal support. In recent times the Church has recovered its sense of community. We are not isolated individuals struggling to cope. We have been made for one another and we need the love and support of each other to live our lives to the full.

Love

We cannot speak about human relationships without speaking about love. I refer here not just to our ability to fall in love and even to live happy, faithful and fruitful lives together, but to "love" as it is defined in the New Testament. This is another realm altogether, where the beloved is everything: where people find fulfilment in service and self-giving. This kind of loving is most severely tested in the midst of pain and suffering and it is here that we find links with sacrifice and redemption.

These are difficult concepts and there is a danger of putting too much emphasis on those texts that seem to suggest that God demands retribution from his Son for all the failures of humankind. But as we shall see there are many ways of understanding the passion and death of Jesus. While the letter to the Hebrews in particular does put stress on the idea of satisfaction being made for sin, its chief concern is to establish for us connections with the Old Testament's understanding of sacrifice and see Jesus as the fulfilment of everything. For richer insights into all this we need to turn to the meditations in John's Gospel and letters, which suggest that Jesus simply could not and would not give up on love and literally loved us to death.

The fact is that we do live in a world full of suffering. For those of us with faith in Jesus, our sufferings and deaths can have real meaning because they can be linked with the suffering and death of Jesus himself. Are the heroic deaths of people like Maximilian Kolbe, who so nobly offered his own life in place of a fellow prisoner in Auschwitz, meaningless, or do they lift us to another plane which defies scientific analysis?

Atheists will insist that we do not need God to give meaning to our lives, and will invite us to share their adult view that "our life is as meaningful, as full and as wonderful as we choose to make it".[4] That of course is all very well for the person who has grown to maturity with all his or her faculties intact, who has formed strong and lasting relationships and enjoyed a successful and rewarding career. But what of the millions who, for whatever reason, have not or cannot? Presumably they have to be sacrificed as a sad statistic on the journey of human evolution.

Learning from experience

Coping with pain and suffering in its many forms is part and parcel of everyone's life. As I look back on my own life, I can only draw conclusions from my experience, which tells me that the God of love revealed in Jesus of Nazareth has touched my life, and the lives of many of those who have been part of mine, to the point where I can say with real conviction that my faith is not theoretical but is born of that experience. And, more than that, it has been tested on occasion by disappointments and suffering.

Looking around and seeing what so many people have to endure, I would certainly not wish to exaggerate the problems I have faced in my own life, but as with all challenges they have been real and they have had to be lived through. What is important about the times of suffering

---

4 Dawkins, *The God Delusion*, p. 404.

is that they also provide us with opportunities. After a breakdown in health at the end of 1988 I learnt a lot about myself and my relationship with God and with others. Later I will explore that time a little because I believe it enabled me to grow in understanding and compassion and prepared me for a whole range of new ministries. More recently I was confronted with another unexpected challenge after a breakdown of trust in my relationship with my religious superiors, which means that I now know something of what people must experience when they are made redundant. I realise that those of us who are members of religious orders are protected from some of the problems that can overwhelm people in the day-to-day struggles of life, and that the paradox of our vow of poverty is that we are largely freed from financial anxiety, which can be crippling for so many people. But of course we have other challenges and we live with the same range of emotions as everyone else. The pain of living with breakdowns in relationships and with division is something few people can avoid completely. This book is essentially about how we allow God to heal us and help us move on to fulfilment. During my times of crisis I have often reflected on the fact that even in apostolic times the Christian community was not spared such conflict and relationships became strained to breaking point. I began this introduction with Paul and Barnabas putting "fresh heart into the disciples". That was in chapter fourteen of the Acts of the Apostles. In chapter fifteen we read that they had "a violent quarrel" (15:39). They then "parted company" and there is no indication that they ever worked together again. So I console myself with the reminder that often we can only leave ourselves and others patiently with the Lord and leave the healing and the solution to him.

Cardinal John Henry Newman wrote a beautiful prayer that encapsulates what I would want to say:

> God has created me to do him some definite service; he has committed some work to me which he has not committed to another. I have my mission – I may never know it in this life, but I shall be told it in the next.
>
> I am a link in a chain, a bond of connection between persons. He has not created me for naught. I shall do good; I shall do his work. I shall be an angel of peace, a preacher of truth in my own place while not intending it – if I do but keep his commandments. Therefore I will trust him. Whatever, wherever I am, I can never be thrown

away. If I am in sickness, my sickness may serve him; in perplexity, my perplexity may serve him. He does nothing in vain. He knows what he is about. He may take away my friends; he may throw me among strangers; he may make me feel desolate, make my spirits sink, hide my future from me – still he knows what he is about.[5]

The message that I believe and have been proclaiming is that at the heart of the Gospel is compassion and forgiveness and that in Christ we and the whole of creation are being reconciled to God. The material I have been using both in my regular ministry and on missions and retreats has developed since the summers at Creighton University between 1989 and 1991, and for a long time I have promised myself that I would assemble the material in book form. Recently I have had the time and opportunity to try to piece it together. So, if these reflections give "fresh heart" and some encouragement to those of you who read them now, then this time will have been especially blessed.

A word of thanks

It is at times of disappointment and difficulty that we are forced to consider again the challenge of Jesus that where our treasure is, there will our hearts be also (Luke 12:34). Such times provide opportunities for refining and purifying ourselves, for realising again that we cannot spend our lives depending primarily on human approval. At the same time, as I have already noted, we are not called to live in isolation. We are part of the great human family and as Christians part of the body of Christ. St Paul began his letters with prayers and thanksgivings and I would like to end this introduction with a word of thanks to family and friends, who include Redemptorist confrères, fellow priests and religious, parishioners and the entire staff at Redemptorist Publications. During the struggles your love and affection, your reassurance and encouragement have sustained me. Many of you have also urged me to complete this project. To you all I dedicate this book. It is time for a new beginning and to take fresh heart.

---

5 *Meditations and Devotions,* Part III: Meditations on Christian Doctrine §1 ("Hope in God – Creator"), 1848.

Chapter Two
The importance of the story

The Redemptorists

St Alphonsus Liguori was the founder of the Redemptorists and one of his great passions was that his spiritual sons should preach the Gospel in a language that could be understood by everyone. We are told that there was an occasion when he was listening attentively as a priest gave forth in flowery language, designed to impress rather than move the people to conversion and to the love of God. He is said to have stepped in and had the offending cleric removed from the pulpit, arranging for the sermon to be finished by someone else.

I think it is fair to say that the particular charism or gift of preaching in ordinary everyday language is one that the Redemptorists have retained and protected since the first community was formed in Scala on the Amalfi coast in 1732. The sadness is that over a long period of time and influenced by the prevailing spirituality of the day, alongside this determination and ability to communicate, we developed a reputation for concentrating on hellfire and the dangers of failure rather than on the compassion and love of God. It is true that Alphonsus could spice his sermons with some graphic stories that sound strange to modern Western ears, but his real legacy was that he fought vehemently to defend freedom of conscience against the hard-line Jansenist teaching of his day.[1] Indeed, so dissatisfied was he with the prevailing moral opinions being taught to students for the priesthood that he rewrote the moral theology textbooks and insisted that his students learned to reach out in compassion especially to those who were poor and uneducated. The Redemptorists are especially proud that throughout the second half of the twentieth century Father Bernard Häring continued that Alphonsian tradition by writing a moral theology that was born of his experience,

---

1 Jansenism was a heresy based on the teachings of a Dutch theologian, Cornelius Jansen, which infected a lot of moral teaching especially in the seventeenth and eighteenth centuries, but traces of it lingered long after that. It called for high moral standards but, by concluding that only a few "elect" would be saved, left many people in a state of hopelessness. Although it had been condemned as heretical before the time of St Alphonsus, its influence was still considerable.

above all as a prisoner during the Second World War. He had joined the German army as a chaplain, but was taken prisoner by the Russians. Throughout his life he continued to revise his work, eventually replacing his original three-volume work, *The Law of Christ*, with three more volumes under the title *Free and Faithful in Christ*.[2] He was among the experts who made a major contribution to the Second Vatican Council.

I like to think that the present generation of Redemptorists have reclaimed that true spirit of Alphonsus and have established a kinder, gentler image within the Church. For me, it has been a joy and a privilege to live in these times, for I have witnessed for myself something of the transition. As a boy, living near the Redemptorist parish in Clapham, south London, I recall at times being unnerved listening to some of those powerful sermons, especially when the missioners were in town, but I also remember countering this in my own mind by reflecting on what kind, friendly, humorous and happy people the priests and brothers seemed to be in themselves. This above all was what attracted me to try my vocation in the Congregation when I finished my secondary schooling at the age of eighteen.

God's story and our stories

Now, having reached that age when one can acquire a senior railcard, I find myself more and more looking back over the past and trying to see the hand of God in the unfolding story of my life, and whenever I am invited to preach a mission or retreat today that is my starting point. Just as Alphonsus and Bernard Häring developed their understanding of the spiritual life and the call to ministry in the light of their experience and the circumstances in which they found themselves, so it will be for you and for me. Our stories matter and have value because, to put it very simply, they are part of God's story. Once we begin to grasp the extraordinary revelation in the book of Genesis that we have been made in the image of God (Genesis 1:27), we have taken the first step in putting together the jigsaw puzzle of our lives.

When we begin to delve into the scriptures we become aware of the importance not just of our own personal stories but also of the stories

---

2 B. Häring, *The Law of Christ*, 3 vols (Cork: Mercier, 1963–67); *Free and Faithful in Christ*, 3 vols (Slough: St Paul Publications, 1978–81).

of the different nations and races – indeed the story of the whole of humankind. We are not isolated individuals struggling alone to make sense of what is going on. We belong to one another and shape the history of the world together.

The Jewish people have always been deeply conscious of their common heritage and their special relationship with God. Their ancient story is vividly portrayed in all the books of the Old Testament. Indeed throughout most of the Old Testament we detect that the people had little or no notion of a personal salvation: as God's chosen people they understood salvation as the preservation of the nation and God's protection of them as a people. Only in the books written nearer to the time of the coming of Jesus do we see a growing awareness of an afterlife and the possibility of personal salvation. For example in the second book of Maccabees, written in the last part of the second century before Christ, we read about atonement being made for sin and the passage concludes: "For if he had not expected the fallen to rise again it would have been superfluous and foolish to pray for the dead" (12:44).[3]

From the outset I suggest it is good to try to get a balanced perspective on the personal and community aspects of the spiritual life, for, as we shall see, they are not mutually exclusive but should interact in such a way that both the individual and the community can flourish together.

To begin with, who we are and where we come from is important. God knows us by name and knows what we are about. Spiritual writers recommend Psalm 138 (139)[4] as a good text for beginners to learn the art of meditation. It begins:

> O Lord, you search me and you know me,
> you know my resting and my rising,
> you discern my purpose from afar.
> You mark when I walk or lie down,
> all my ways lie open to you.
> Before ever a word is on my tongue
> you know it, O Lord, through and through.

---

3 It is worth noting that the books of Maccabees are not part of the Jewish canon of scripture.

4 Please note that the numbering of some of the psalms in the Greek version of the Bible differs from the Hebrew version. Where appropriate in this book, the Hebrew numbering is given in brackets.

This is not the all-seeing eye of a God who is watching over us to catch us out should we do wrong, but the loving and protective eye of a parent who is concerned for our welfare and wants only the best for us. For those of us who were blessed with good and loving parents this is easier to grasp than for those whose lives may have been scarred by unhappy homes and childhoods. But, no matter what our backgrounds, all our lives will have been a mixture of joys and sorrows from an early age. Of course the question does arise as to how much we are conditioned by our circumstances and experiences. For those of us who have been in pastoral ministry for any length of time, it is evident that people's behaviour can often be explained and even excused in the light of what they have had to endure, but by the same token that is not to suggest that we are so conditioned as to be unable to make free choices. I remember a priest defending the notion of original sin at a baptism by saying to the parents: "Should you be uncertain about the truth of this matter, your doubts will disappear the first time your child stamps his foot and says, 'I won't.'"

The message at the heart of this book is that no matter what our temperament, what our circumstances, what we have done, how we feel about ourselves, everything is redeemable because of Jesus of Nazareth. When we begin to meditate, I believe the more we know about ourselves, the more receptive we will be to this message of the Gospel, the good news that can override and make sense of all the bad news in our own lives and in the world around us. For some people the task of getting to know themselves includes the relentless pursuit of their family tree: a desire to know who were their ancestors, what was their human stock.

Jesus enters our story

Interestingly both Matthew and Luke go to a lot of trouble to provide us with genealogies of Jesus. Matthew opens the Gospel with his genealogy and traces the Jesus story back to Abraham, cleverly contriving to provide three sets of fourteen generations until he arrives at the birth of Jesus (1:17). By contrast Luke begins with Jesus and works back all the way to Adam; and his genealogy comes in chapter three, after Jesus is baptised and as he is about to begin his public ministry. Spiritual writers and scripture commentators take delight in pointing out all the rogues and unsavoury types who appear in these lists and it is certainly an interesting study to trace their different stories through the Old Testament. After all even David, who began the royal line that would give us the Messiah, compounded his sin of adultery with murder (see 2 Samuel 11–12).[5] For our purposes it is enough to note that both Matthew and Luke are at pains to reveal the truly human origins of Jesus. He really was a human being and like the rest of us had his family tree.

In his Gospel John is likewise at pains to establish the humanity of Jesus: "The Word was made flesh, he lived among us" (1:14). Of course all four Gospels also go to great lengths to remind us that Jesus was at the same time truly God; and here John leads the way with his opening sentence: "In the beginning was the Word: the Word was with God and the Word was God." In a later chapter we will come back to the question of the relationship between the humanity and the divinity of Christ – what theologians call the hypostatic union – and moreover how we in turn share in his divinity by becoming children of God, but for now I want to dwell on the significance of Christ's humanity and our humanity. I am grateful that modern spirituality has emphasised again the importance of realising that Jesus was truly human, for it is only when we grasp the full weight of what is said in the letter to the Hebrews – "For it is not as if we had a high priest who was incapable of feeling our weaknesses with us; but we have one who has been tempted in every way that we are, though he is without sin" (4:15) – that we can, I believe, develop a personal relationship with him.

To explore this a little further: I need to remind myself to speak in the present about Jesus' humanity. It is not simply that he was a man two thousand years ago. If I think like that I am in danger of thinking that God simply took possession of a human body for around thirty years. The whole point of the resurrection is that Christ retained his humanity – now his glorified humanity – and that glory is our destiny. I would suggest therefore that if we are truly to develop a relationship with Jesus it will be because we get to know him personally and, as with every relationship, in the process we will get to know ourselves too. It is when we know for certain that Jesus keeps with us the promise he made to the apostles, "I am with you always" (Matthew 28:20), that we can truly begin to see our story as part of God's story.

---

5   In his book *Loved for Who I Am* (pp. 76-82), Cardinal Carlo Maria Martini provides a masterly meditation on the story of David, Bathsheba and Uriah (Chawton: Redemptorist Publications, 2000).

At the beginning of a retreat I invite the participants to spend some time thinking about their stories and trying to identify those moments when they recognise the hand of God in their lives, hopefully helping them to put the jigsaw together and see the connections, with a view to discerning where the Lord wishes to lead them next.

Just as I need to know that Jesus is truly human and truly understands my experiences, so it is important for me to communicate to the listener that I have an empathy and a sympathy for them in their varied circumstances. Remember how in Hebrews we are told this about Jesus:

> It was essential that he should in this way become completely like his brothers [and sisters] so that he could be a compassionate and trustworthy high priest of God's religion, able to atone for human sins. That is, because he has himself been through temptation he is able to help others who are tempted. (2:17-18)

So, just as to understand Jesus we want and need to know his story, I will need to share some of my story if I am to communicate how I know and have experienced Christ's love for me. After all, Mary's Magnificat is presented to us by Luke so that the words can be put on our lips too: "My soul proclaims the greatness of the Lord and my spirit exults in God my saviour; because he has looked upon his lowly handmaid… for the Almighty has done great things for me" (1:46-49). Of course a delicate balance needs to be struck in judging how much to say, but a willingness to share especially the more painful parts of our stories can sometimes prove the catalyst for releasing others to discover or renew their faith in Christ. In the next chapter I will summarise how my story has unfolded, but for now I will offer just one story to illustrate this point.

I have mentioned a breakdown in health at the end of 1988. It took me some time to regain any confidence but eventually, when giving retreats, I decided to include some reference to those events as part of the story that had shaped me, not least because in doing so I was able to highlight other significant moments in the story, which had shaped my understanding of life and the Gospel. During the mid 1990s I was giving a retreat to the small community of Loreto sisters in Gibraltar and after a couple of days I invited the sisters to reflect on their stories and look for connections that would help them to see their stories as part of God's story. In that context I chose to tell them a little of my story. I ended by saying: "So you see I don't believe any of us has it all sewn up: we spend our lives searching, trying to understand and always waiting on God." That evening Sister Patricia came to see me, expressing her immense gratitude but really making me sit up and think. She said: "I really am relieved that you gave that conference this evening, because for the first couple of days you spoke with such confidence that I got the impression that you had got it all sewn up. Indeed I was wondering how on earth I would be able to share any of my misgivings and concerns with you."

From that day I have been careful to reveal the vulnerable side of myself early on in my encounters with any retreat group, and Patricia and I have become great friends. From the relative comfort of Gibraltar she chose to ask her superiors for permission to go to Peru and work among those in desperate need of education and much more besides. We keep in touch and from afar I watch in admiration as she sends me photographs of schools rising up in the midst of seeming wasteland. Always she is surrounded by dozens of radiantly happy little faces. In their own way they are the greatest testimony to me of the truth of the Gospel and I thank God for Patricia and the countless wonderful men and women of faith it has been my privilege to meet.

Chapter Three
The background to my story

My family

These days if you are invited to address a conference or a seminar group, it is usual to be asked for a few biographical notes. These might be used by whoever moderates the session by way of introducing you before you speak, and/or they may be included in a conference brochure. I find it helpful to know something about where speakers are coming from: it often gives the clue as to why they approach their subject in the way they do. By the same token when they offer opinions that are unexpected it challenges my inevitable inbuilt prejudices. In turn when I have found myself in unfamiliar settings, sometimes I have sensed the prejudices of those who have already marked my card because I am a Catholic priest or a Redemptorist or both.

I think it is good to invite retreatants to take time at the beginning of their journey to look back on their lives and see the hand of God at work, and so I hope the reader will indulge me if I give a summary of where I am coming from. I hope it will help to clarify the way I have learnt to understand and share the Gospel of Jesus of Nazareth.

As far as I can tell my family was fairly typical of so many whose Catholic roots can be found in Ireland, although my father, who was born in Newport (then Monmouthshire) in 1897, never actually set foot in Ireland. He had considered a vocation to the priesthood himself and was educated by the Rosminians at Ratcliffe College in Leicestershire.[1] The First World War rudely interrupted his education and he joined the South Wales Borderers as a young man of seventeen, suffering some fearful experiences in Greece and eventually being invalided home. It was clear that he carried the scars of those dreadful times all his life and for the last twenty years or so he needed barbiturates to calm the tension that left him with regular palpitation attacks. For all the tension that this

---

1 The Rosminians are members of the Institute of Charity, a religious order founded by Antonio Rosmini in 1828. They have nine parishes in England and Wales, as well as Ratcliffe College.

sometimes caused in the home, we had a wonderful relationship. He was old enough to be my grandfather but he shared with me his love of sport and his ability to keep things in perspective especially when faced with a crisis. For example, I remember being immensely proud of him when he calmly dealt with a man whose behaviour caused everyone else on the London Underground to look the other way.

Eventually dad settled in London and worked for the Civil Service, where he met my mother, whom he simply worshipped. After mum's death in 2002 I stumbled across some wonderfully affectionate letters dad had written to her when they were courting. Mum was sixteen years younger and also working in the Civil Service. They were planning to marry, but now the Second World War intervened. Dad wanted to go back into the army but he was too old. He always insisted he got the worst deal of all: the trenches in the First World War and the Blitz in London in the Second. Eventually they married in the autumn of 1941 and a year later my sister, Anne, was born. While I was generally her pestilential little brother when we were younger, our friendship has blossomed over the years and we have rejoiced with each other during the good times and supported each other through the bad.

I was born in the autumn of 1946, one of the boom babies after the Second World War. Mum actually gave birth to me in the maisonette in south London where I was to live all my life until going to the Redemptorist novitiate in 1964.[2] My father, meticulous to detail, used to enjoy telling the story of how he insisted that my birth be recorded as the day before the one suggested by the midwife: he had heard the first cries at ten to midnight!

It is easy to look back nostalgically on our past and see it through the proverbial rose-tinted spectacles, but I have no doubt that Anne and I were extremely fortunate. We were blessed with two loving parents who made great sacrifices to ensure that we were brought up and educated in a loving and stable home. Money was scarce – we still joke that dad's

---

2 When giving a retreat to the Clifton clergy at Downside Abbey in the summer of 2004, I could not resist quoting from the *Daily Mail*, which had referred to the estate where I was brought up as "the tough Larkhall estate in Lambeth, South London". They were reporting on a young lad from the same housing complex, who had not been performing well at his local school and who had been taken on as an experiment by Downside School. A television series documented his progress. Although he did outstandingly well both academically and at sport, sadly it did not work out in the end. The *Daily Mail* article was written prior to the documentary and after he had been suspended for stealing a mobile phone (James Mills and Charlotte Gill, *Daily Mail*, Wednesday 12th March 2003, p. 21).

refrain was always "we can't afford it" – but every year he ensured that we had a week or two at the coast and there were the annual treats, the pantomime and circus during the Christmas holidays, and sundry visits to zoos and museums, not to mention the hours spent at the Oval cricket ground watching my beloved Surrey County Cricket Club and even my first football match, Chelsea versus Sunderland in the spring of 1958. I had started supporting Sunderland a few years before after listening to a match on the radio and have remained faithful to this day. When it came to rugby, dad's game, his Irish roots took over and he convinced me that the Irish with their limited resources played the game as it really should be played, with an expansive freedom. I loved going to the Changing of the Guard and Trooping the Colour: the sound of a military band still manages to send a shiver down my spine. Anne and I were left in no doubt about the heroism of those in the armed services who had made the ultimate sacrifice that we might enjoy the freedom to live in relative peace. With the passing of the years I find myself more and more convinced that the Gospel calls us to a more radical solution to all conflict and that violence is hard to justify in any circumstances, but I know it is easy to be simplistic and I have never taken the absolutist stand that cannot countenance even the notion of military chaplains. Over the years I have valued the opportunity to work with the chaplains and personnel of the three armed services.

Our Catholicism was like the air we breathed. Mum had been instructed in the Catholic faith by a Rosminian and received into the Church at St Etheldreda's, Ely Place, before my parents' marriage at the Redemptorist church in Clapham. I was baptised at Ely Place and because of dad's connections with the Rosminians we occasionally went there for Mass on Sunday, but generally we went to Corpus Christi, Maiden Lane, the delightful little church just off the Strand, near the old Covent Garden market. We started going there because dad was working just off the Strand and sometimes went to the lunchtime Benedictions.[3] It was at Maiden Lane that I served on the altar for the best part of ten years and my sister sang in the choir. It is known as the actors' church, being close to the West End. Gigli, the great operatic tenor, is famously said to have joined the choir for Mass one Sunday and given an impromptu concert on the steps afterwards.

---

3 Those were the days before the reforms of Vatican II and even before the fasting for Holy Communion from midnight had been reduced, first to three hours and then to just one hour.

At home both mum and dad prayed with us. In those days this was fairly formal, but we learnt more than just the standard prayers. Even as a child I warmed to this beautiful version of the Compline prayer: "Visit, we beseech thee, O Lord, this house and family and drive far from it all the snares of the enemy. May your holy angels dwell here to keep us in peace and may your blessing be always upon us, through Christ our Lord. Amen."[4] The idea that angels were among us was comforting and appealed to me. The only problem was that while I was keen on my guardian angel protecting me, I was not so keen that the same angel might be watching when I was up to no good, and of course this applied even more to the God who knew everything. Now I do not want to decry all the catechesis of a bygone age and bemoan the guilt-ridden state of Catholics of a certain generation, but there is no doubt that psychologically those early impressions and images were bound to have left their mark on us no matter how much we have tried to mature in our spiritual understanding and religious practice.

Schooldays

My first three years at school were with the La Retraite sisters at St Anselm's in Tooting and it was at St Anselm's that I made my First Communion at the age of seven. Then I went to St Joseph's College, Beulah Hill, the oldest foundation of the De La Salle brothers in the country. Interestingly, when we are looking for connections, the brothers received hospitality from the Redemptorists when they first came to Britain and the site of the first college was in Clapham's Old Town. I have no horror stories to tell about my schooling. The style was very different and having worked with young people a lot as a priest I sometimes wish I could have enjoyed the benefits of some of the modern methods of education. They seem to make learning so much more interesting and so much more fun and often youngsters seem to have a better rapport with their teachers. But I note also the other side of the coin, a widespread concern about lack of discipline, perhaps the result of overfamiliarity. Like virtually all the active religious orders in this part of the world the brothers now have very few new vocations, but

---

4   Jane Williams has written a wonderful little book called *Angels* (Oxford: Lion, 2006),
    which I would commend to all those who want to revive their childhood memories,
    develop their understanding and see the angels in their proper biblical settings.

I have remained in touch with some of them and was privileged to be invited to lead a retreat at Clayton Court, their retirement home in the south of England, in September 2001. Suffice it to say that it was good to have them sitting and listening to me for a change, but I was very kind to them!

I do not think my school days were the happiest days of my life, but neither did I loathe them. I made some wonderful friends with whom I have kept in touch all my life and we had lots of fun. I still recall those idyllic times when the exams were over and the summer holidays had arrived and we were free, with seemingly not a care in the world, just free to play cricket or tennis or whatever the sport of the moment happened to be. The Latin version of Psalm 42 (43), which the priest recited at the beginning of the Tridentine Mass, and which dad helped me to master when I was learning to be a server, was framed by verse four. The priest would pray, "Introibo ad altare Dei", to which the server would reply: "Ad Deum qui laetificat juventutem meam." My old missal translated this: "I will go in unto the altar of God; unto God who giveth joy to my youth." In recent months I have gone back to begin each day with that refrain, asking the Lord to help me recover the joy of my youth. I assure you this is not a vain nostalgic search for something long lost, but the genuine belief that God always wants the best for us. Joy comes with freedom and the knowledge that we are already the children of God (see 1 John 3:1-2). I will come back to this theme later in the book because I am convinced that one of our primary tasks is to enable one another to live fulfilled and fruitful lives, experiencing the truth that we are already redeemed by Christ. It is the conviction that in the midst of all the turmoil of life it is possible to live knowing that, as Dame Julian of Norwich so beautifully put it, "all will be well".

If there were halcyon days in my youth, there were also plenty of anxieties. You will have gathered that I retain a great affection for my father, but on one matter in particular I have come to question his opinion. Generally he was very understanding, but I guess the bitter experience of the First World War had much to do with his having to grow up very quickly, so whenever he saw that I was worried he would insist that when I grew up I would know what real worries were all about. However, my experience suggests that children's worries are just as serious as adults' worries and indeed can sometimes be even more alarming because as a child you do not have the experience to put your worries into perspective. At an early age I became quite scrupulous, fearful that I was out of favour with God. My temperament was such that I hated being out of favour with anyone and always sought to put matters right as quickly as possible, though in fairness not at any cost. Lying, cheating or stealing were never real temptations for me. For example, I just knew that I could not live with myself if I cheated to win. But alongside that was a keenly competitive spirit. Looking back I think it probably had much to do with an attempt to establish myself, for I was never a high-flyer either academically or on the sporting field. I have often joked that the prizes I won were for things like "application", while when it came to sport I did captain the second eleven cricket team but never played for the first.

A good example of how scruples were beginning to bother me at an early age was my behaviour on my confirmation day. I was twelve and the De La Salle brothers had us at fever pitch in readiness for the occasion. I do not know whether it was a cunning ruse, but the rumour was circulating that recently Archbishop Cowderoy had refused to confirm a group of children because they had not known the answers to his questions,[5] so on top of my anxiety about whether I was in a state of grace came the added burden that I might let the whole school down on the night in question. In the event all went well. However, prior to the ceremony we had been the given the afternoon off and, while most of my pals were probably playing football, I took myself off to St Mary's, Clapham. Even though I had been to confession only a few days before, I summoned a priest to hear my confession again and ensure that I would not be committing some kind of sacrilege.

There were some wonderfully gentle priests in the Clapham community in those days, but there were also one or two who were less than sympathetic even with a confused child. I remember one Saturday afternoon wandering around Clapham Common in a daze after being shouted at and I will never forget my mother's distress when she returned after a bad experience too. So I learnt to be choosy about to whom I confessed my sins and years later I remember secretly applauding Cardinal Hume when I heard him address a large group from the Association of Separated and Divorced Catholics and advise them to seek out and discuss their problems with a *sympathetic* priest.

---

5 Cyril Cowderoy was the Archbishop of Southwark and it was customary in those days for the bishop to ask the children questions about the faith and the sacrament of confirmation to ensure that they had been properly instructed.

I like to think that I have always been gentle as a confessor. Scruples are not as common today as they were but they are not entirely a thing of the past and my own experiences certainly prepared me to respond to those troubled with the affliction. One of the secrets in being able to engage scrupulous people is to be able accurately to predict what they might be about to say next, or what might occur to them only after they have left you. Once they know that you really do understand there is a better chance that they will accept your advice. In an age of non-directive counselling they are always candidates for clear spiritual direction. Fortunately my own scruples never really got the better of me: indeed when I was a Redemptorist novice and student I used to be teased by my peers that I always eventually found a way round them.

In all of us there is an instinctive common sense which keeps calling us to keep things in perspective: if we lose that we are in trouble. Nevertheless I will always remain indebted to Stephen Naidoo – later to become Archbishop of Cape Town. For a few years he was my confessor when I was a student and quietly led me into calmer waters. As an addendum on this subject, St Alphonsus was plagued with scruples all his life but proved to be the most wonderful counsellor to those who came to him with the same problem. In this he was the perfect example of the wounded healer.

A vocation to the Redemptorists

When it comes to children, I think the teaching Church needs to think again very seriously about how we prepare them for the sacrament of reconciliation, and how and where we celebrate it with them. Indeed I think the whole question of the sacrament of reconciliation needs careful reconsideration. It is something I will offer some thoughts on towards the end of the book. For now I would simply say that when children and young people do approach this sacrament, it provides wonderful opportunities for the priest, by his whole demeanour and attitude, to demonstrate the overwhelming love, concern and compassion of Jesus.

It is so important to take children seriously and give them good spiritual experiences. Of course this applies not just in regard to the sacrament of reconciliation but to everything. Again I can fall back on my own experience to illustrate the point. Most of us will be able to recall key moments when our lives were given new purpose or direction, and often they arise from ordinary and seemingly insignificant encounters. One such encounter for me was at St Mary's, Clapham. It was during the holidays and I often served a weekday Mass in the early morning. Those were the days before concelebration and priests in the community not appointed for a public Mass would celebrate so-called private Masses at the many side altars around the church. There was an army of young lads willing to serve. They were different days, but you should not be misled into thinking that we were overly pious. Indeed at seven in the morning when virtually all the side altars would be in use we were like jockeys, hoping to get the fastest priest and return to the sacristy first and therefore triumphant!

On the morning before the day in question old Brother Anselm, the sacristan, asked me what I was planning to do when I grew up and I knew it would please him if I said I wanted to be a priest, so I did. The following morning, on cue, a young, newly ordained priest, Father Frank Dickinson – the same Father Dickinson with whom I was to be in community some fifty years later – singled me out and checked as to whether I was the young man wanting to become a priest. He took me past the great oak door, and showed me around the monastery, which also housed the early offices of Redemptorist Publications. It was not the conversation that left its mark on me – though I do recall encountering Father Dickinson's wry sense of humour for the first time – it was the fact that someone had taken an interest in me and taken me seriously. I remember running the mile home to break the news to the family. Later, when I was vocations director for over seven years in the 1970s, I tried to remember that lesson in welcoming the boys and young men who showed an interest in our way of life.

The result of my meeting with Father Dickinson was that I became part of a vocations group, which met each year after Easter and visited the students at Hawkstone Hall in Shropshire, the seminary of the London Province.[6] I was grateful that there was never any suggestion that I should go to the Junior Seminary in Birmingham: the Redemptorists

---

6 The Redemptorists now name their provinces after the principal city where they are located. The London Province covers the whole of England, Scotland and Wales, although now there is no longer a Redemptorist community in Wales. The whole of Ireland forms a separate province: the Dublin Province. The Redemptorist seminary was at Hawkstone Park from 1926 until 1973, when the students moved to Canterbury. From the early part of the twenty-first century our students now study at the national seminary in Scotland.

were obviously satisfied that I was getting a good enough education with the De La Salle brothers. At school my focus was sufficiently on the priesthood for me to decide to opt for the Arts rather than the Sciences and to struggle on with Latin, which in those days was still regarded as a prerequisite, and somehow I managed to scrape an A level in it, but overall my results would not have landed me a place at university. However, the Redemptorists seemed pleased to take me into the novitiate and off I went to St Mary's, Kinnoull, Perth, the first monastery to have been built in Scotland after the Reformation. The story goes that on a visit to Perth Queen Victoria asked about the magnificent building on the hillside and was astutely assured that it was the mental hospital, which in fact lay a few hundred yards to the east!

Novitiate

After all the stress of studying for exams and striving to hold one's own in the rough and tumble of a large school, I found the novitiate a liberating experience. There were plenty of strange and even bizarre customs to get used to, but somehow there was a feeling that everyone was rooting for you and I began to discover a confidence I had never had at school. The young lad who had been terrified of being asked to read in class, now found himself enjoying the challenge of reading in the refectory during meals and even having the temerity to challenge the novice master when being corrected over a pronunciation, though that was not a wise move! We kept remarkably fit, walking for miles across some spectacular countryside every week, and even managing the odd game of football and cricket. Most of the year there were twelve of us, seven choir novices with the priesthood in mind and five wanting to become brothers.

Seminary

After our profession in October 1965 the seven of us headed off to Hawkstone Park and brought the number of students in the seminary to forty-five. A couple of years earlier it had reached a high point of forty-nine, but by the time I was finishing in 1971 the dramatic erosion that struck most religious orders was beginning to bite and serious consideration was being given to abandoning Hawkstone and linking up with another establishment. Such a move would also provide the opportunity of linking into the mainstream of tertiary education in the country. It was one of the sad lacks of Hawkstone that after six years of study we had no official qualifications. I must confess at the time that did not bother me and unlike many of my contemporaries I enjoyed my years in the heart of the Shropshire countryside. There is no doubt that our education there was extremely limited, but it is always easy to lay the blame on those responsible for the system. Many of us failed to use our initiative and seize the opportunities that did exist. That era did produce some remarkably gifted and committed priests who have given the Church outstanding service in different parts of the world. An obvious example would be Bishop Kevin Dowling, the Bishop of Rustenburg in South Africa. In 2006, his confrères in South Africa marked his fifteen years as a bishop by publishing a book of essays particularly focusing on his efforts to alleviate the devastating effects of the HIV/AIDS pandemic. He is regarded as having followed in the footsteps of his legendary cousin, Archbishop Denis Hurley, in promoting the causes of justice and peace in southern Africa.[7]

One thing that Hawkstone did achieve for me was the realisation that the Second Vatican Council was calling for a much more radical rethink of what it means to be Christian than had widely been envisaged or expected. We witnessed the tension as some of our younger men returned from further studies in Rome and began to teach alongside the established team of lectors. I was excited because I could see that much that I had found confusing or simply suspended judgement on was now up for discussion. Problems were being identified and sometimes resolved. There was a refreshingly new atmosphere of openness and dialogue. Undoubtedly one of the most important was the changed atmosphere in ecumenical relations and the fact the Catholic Church now wished to enter into dialogue with the other Christian traditions. As this story unfolds you will see why this meant and still means so much to me and I will conclude this chapter with a story about my mother, which illustrates it very personally. But first I will complete the quick sweep of the overall story.

---

7   Andrew T. Burns CSsR and Seán Wales CSsR (eds), *Your Servant for Jesus' Sake: Essays in Honour of Bishop Kevin Dowling CSsR* (Merrivale: Redemptorist Pastoral Publications, 2006).

Early years of ministry

There was a huge sense of expectation among those of us who had stayed the course and were ordained in the early 1970s. I enjoyed a wonderful first year out of the seminary in our parish in Plymouth from the autumn of 1971. Father Gerry Costello, the parish priest, was a gentle character who gave me my head and heaps of support and encouragement. He had long since put life in perspective, having landed on D-Day on Juno Beach in Normandy as chaplain of 48 Commando of the Royal Marines. He was rightly proud of the fact that he was a fully fledged marine with his green beret. At the end of that year I moved to Kinnoull in Scotland to join our mission team. There was no shortage of work, for as well as the missions in the parishes some of our younger men had been experimenting with missions in the large secondary schools. We were on the road most of the time. Father Vincent Lucas, the rector, was convinced that psychologically it was better to have his men fully employed and was famous for his saying: "Keep them out, keep them happy." So much for what traditionally had been believed to be the ideal balance for a Redemptorist missioner of half the year at home attending to the spiritual life; we were not fazed, for it was encouraging in those early days to feel wanted, and if I may put it crudely we were playing to packed houses and receiving a great deal of affirmation. Even the school missions, some of them in the tough inner cities, were going well, for we had struck on a formula that engaged the youngsters and got a response. By the time I moved to Sunderland in late 1973 I was full of enthusiasm for the mission scene and delighted to be continuing with the work, this time supporting the one other missioner in the house, Father Terry Creech, but also able to take on work in other parts of the country with other confrères because of my other role as vocations director.

I should not pass over the fact that within the London Province there was a continual struggle among the missioners about how to approach the work. Some of the old guard considered that the well-tried methods that had served generations of parish missioners were being abandoned in favour of nothing more than gimmicks, and we had some explosive exchanges at our annual missioners' meetings. Because of my new-found circumstances I was in the fortunate position of being almost freelance. With the vocations work taking precedence, I was able to choose how many missions I took on and with whom I wanted to give them. Terry and I had formed a happy working relationship, but in 1975

35

he was appointed rector and parish priest in Sunderland and thereafter I often teamed up with confrères who were in specialised ministries like the publications work, but who appreciated the chance to get out a few times a year. Again they were rewarding times and we were able to experiment. Towards the end of that period we even moved beyond the parish/school setting into a couple of universities. This I reckoned to be particularly useful in regard to the vocations work, for by the end of the 1970s it was generally agreed that candidates straight from school should not be the norm.

Erdington Abbey

I moved to Erdington Abbey, Birmingham, in February 1981 to become rector and parish priest. These were exciting times for me. The abbey was then and still is numerically the largest Redemptorist parish in the province. In those days the Sunday Mass attendance averaged over 2,800, baptisms always topped 100 and weddings and funerals over 50 per year. There was a two-form-entry primary school and St Edmund Campion, the Catholic comprehensive across the road, was six-form entry and had its own sixth form. I already knew something about the parish because the previous incumbent, Father Charlie Corrigan, had invited me to lead a mission there in 1977. It was a memorable experience for the six of us who took part, including two of our students.

I worked hard – possibly too hard – immersing myself in the life of the parish. I was well supported by my confrères in the community, which at one point was fifteen strong, although only three were officially assigned to the parish. Understandably as a young man I was keen to make my mark, to ensure that the wonderful spirit inherited from my predecessors was not lost. I was concerned that the abbey parish should be a model parish with a real sense of mission. The Rite of Christian Initiation of Adults (RCIA) was introduced and I went out of my way to establish a good working relationship with the other Christian churches in the area. For example, on my first Good Friday we had such a remarkable response from the abbey parish to boost the walk of witness through "the village" that the police refused to let the procession begin until they had called for reinforcements. I found myself fulfilled with my ministry, which was interesting and varied. When I had completed my six years and it was time to move on I was able to look back with immense gratitude and a feeling of satisfaction, but I had not anticipated the trouble that was brewing.

Getting to know ourselves is obviously a life's work and I have valued the opportunities to look at different personality types with a view to understanding myself better and learning how to live healthily. People vary in how much store they put by programmes like the Enneagram.[8] I certainly do not think they should become new gospels, but it seems clear to me that we are very different and the more we understand what makes us tick, the better we can learn how to relate to one another and deal with our own demons. I realised and everyone else confirmed that on the Enneagram I am typical of the personality that is categorised as a perfectionist and is summed up as follows:

> They are conscientious with a strong moral sense of right and wrong. They are organised, disciplined and critical if their perfectionist standards are not met. However, they can be impatient and resentful with repressed anger lurking beneath the surface.[9]

The Enneagram proposes that, whichever of its nine personality types people belong to, they can live either healthily or unhealthily. The theory is that each type has two wings – these wings being other personality types – towards which each of our types will inevitably veer. Veering towards or cultivating one of these wings will lead to healthy living, going towards the other to unhealthy living. In retrospect it seems clear to me that after I left Erdington I spiralled towards my unhealthy wing and became self-preoccupied and quite depressed. My unhealthy wing is summarised as follows:

> They are sensitive, romantic and emotionally honest. They view their experiences as opportunities for growth. They need to express themselves usually through some form of art. Hypersensitive or self-indulgent, they are prone to melancholy, envy or withdrawing into themselves.

In a nutshell, I think the problem was that I do like order and clarity in my life. I feel comfortable when I know that I have completed a task

---

8 The Enneagram is a psychological system which designates nine basic personality types.

9 The summaries of these personality types were taken from the website of Usha Mullan: <http://www.ushamullan.com> accessed 11th February 2009.

and can sign it off and feel a sense of achievement. Applying that to an appointment given me by my religious superiors, the challenge was to see through the allotted term to the best of my ability. I had seen through my allotted two terms at Erdington and I was expecting to be moved. However, I had not realised either the toll that those six years had taken on me or quite how emotionally attached I had become to the people and the place. Never before in my Redemptorist life had I put down roots like this and I was ill-prepared for how emotionally fragile I would feel when the round of farewells was over and I had moved on.

St Benet's, Sunderland, and a crisis

My new appointment in May 1987 was to take on the same roles of rector and parish priest in my beloved Sunderland, but somehow I was anxious and nervous at the prospect. To be honest I had already begun to feel the pressure towards the end of my term at Erdington and when I arrived in Sunderland that pressure increased because I sensed a weight of expectation both from outside and from within myself. Because of my time there in the 1970s many of the parishioners knew me and one thing that immediately hit me on my return was my reputation for being able to communicate with the children. On the first morning I walked into the school and was surrounded by children who began to ask if I was the priest who told stories about Freddie Freckles. Somehow my reaction at that moment summed up everything I was feeling: that I simply did not have the energy or enthusiasm to live up to their expectations. I felt drained and anxious. Of course, because of my temperament I drove myself on and tried to live up to what I thought everyone was expecting of me but above all to live up to what I had decided to expect of myself. Ostensibly I think I was covering up reasonably well. Certainly no one seemed to suspect what I was going through and I managed to keep up the pretence for over eighteen months.

By the autumn of 1988 the panic attacks were becoming more frequent and acute and my judgements were becoming more and more erratic. For example, Monsignor Peter Smith, then rector of Wonersh, the seminary in the south of England, later to become Archbishop of Cardiff, had asked me to give a retreat to the students in November 1988. I had decided that it would be good for me to do something different and agreed. However, preparing for that retreat just became another mighty burden and when I arrived in Wonersh on 19th November I recall Peter taking one look at me and asking if I was all right. He suggested that I take it easy at the retreat and if I did not feel up to a conference just to send the students off to pray. However, pride drove me on and somehow I managed to get through the week, missing nothing. It was the same old syndrome: get the job done and enjoy the satisfaction and sense of achievement at the end. One of our confrères, Father Stan Mellett, had a wonderful way of summing up how Redemptorists feel in these situations by telling us that when he returned from a mission or retreat and the other members of the community asked how things had gone, he would respond with: "I think I got away with it again."

Well, I may have got away with it at Wonersh, though I think the more discerning students realised I was more than a little hyped, but I was not to get away with it for much longer. Within a fortnight of returning I collapsed in an emotional heap, this time realising that I just did not have the energy or courage to face Christmas in the parish. I had already spoken to my Provincial, Father Kevin Callaghan, at the end of the retreat in Wonersh and warned him that I was not coping well, and when the crunch came I can only say that I had wonderful support from my confrères and all my family and friends. I have joked since that I had hoped that a couple of weeks in the Bahamas would do the trick, but the Provincial was certain that I should come off the job and have a complete break and I know now that he was right, though I realise I must have been a handful during the first few weeks of my enforced rest. The Franciscan Missionaries of the Divine Motherhood, with whom I had been friends for many years, took me under their wing initially and arranged for me to see a psychiatrist at their hospital in Guildford. I will always be indebted to Noel Lavin, for at our first meeting he got me laughing at myself – the first time I could remember laughing for months – and convinced me that I was not going entirely out of my mind.

Certainly by Easter 1989 I was itching to start doing something again, but everyone was being very protective and it was as much as I could do to get my new community – I was lodging at the publications house in Hampshire – to let me take on the occasional parish supply in the area. The real transformation was to begin that summer because it was then that I went to the United States for a spirituality summer school that was to change my life for good. In his book *Where Does the Jesus*

Story Begin?, Denis McBride intriguingly points out that each of the four Gospels begins the Jesus story in a different place, and not by chance, for each of the evangelists has a different purpose in mind.[10] Illustrating this by inviting us to consider where we would begin our own stories, he recalls that his father always used to tell the family that his life really began on the day he met their mother. If I were to pinpoint a similar moment in my own life it would be that summer of 1989, because as a result of my experiences then I began to see all that had gone before and all that has happened since in a wholly new light. Certainly it has completely transformed my understanding of the meaning of salvation and therefore my own spiritual life and my preaching. It is not that I want to dismiss in any way all that went before: far from it. I believe that the Lord accepted what I managed to offer him in those first forty-three years and as always made up for what was lacking; but one thing became abundantly clear, and it was that I had been relying far too much on my own strength and energy and not nearly enough on the Lord. I had learnt the theory of "letting go and letting God" many years before and I had believed it and preached it, but I had not lived it. Like so many others I found it very difficult really to let go and not be in control, and incidentally I still do. But now, having been forced to let go in a painful set of circumstances, I realise the wonderful liberation that comes from accepting that life is often very messy and that I do not have to get everything sorted.

My new understanding and vision were translated into the message that I now share in conferences, sermons and homilies. As I have indicated, it is the content of these that forms the substance of this book. It is clear to me now that I was baptised and ordained to be nothing other than a witness to the resurrection of Jesus and to play my part in allowing him to heal the brokenness of the world.

I have mentioned the wonderful scripture course of Marty Palmer, but I am also grateful for all the courses I took at Creighton during the summer schools of 1989, 1990 and 1991. Back in England I had begun research into the Church's pastoral care of those who had suffered marital breakdown and so I found myself as a full-time student again. While in some ways this took some getting used to, I believe the fact that I was able to bring twenty years of pastoral experience to the work

---

10 D. McBride, *Where Does the Jesus Story Begin? Reflections on the Beginning of the Gospels* (Chawton: Redemptorist Publications, 2006).

added an extra invaluable dimension to it. I moved to Canterbury to help at the Redemptorist seminary and in due course joined the staff at the Franciscan Study Centre, where our students were studying. These were years with many new challenges, but I found them very rewarding and fulfilling. I remained in Canterbury until my move to the publications house in Hampshire in the autumn of 1999.

My mother's story

Before I close this chapter and move to the material of my retreat conferences I will share as promised a story about my mother, which illustrates what I invite retreatants to do: namely to look for the connections in their lives that reveal to them the presence of God.

I have mentioned that my mother was received into the Catholic Church prior to her wedding to my father. This was not simply a matter of convenience but was a mature and thoughtful decision, part of a faith journey that was deeply edifying, and it was after my mother had died that I was able to piece together the fuller picture. It was only then that I recalled her telling me years before that she had not been baptised until she was a young woman. It was not that her parents were particularly irreligious. They were of old-fashioned Protestant stock: her father was a Duncan from Perth – a loose link there with the Redemptorists – and, from what I could gather, her mother (the only grandparent I ever knew) was somewhat suspicious of the Catholic Church but eventually warmed to my father and became more sympathetic. Anyway, her parents did not have my mother baptised as an infant and when she became a regular churchgoer in her teenage years they persuaded her to wait until she had finished her schooling so that she could make an adult decision, which she duly did at the age of eighteen.

I had forgotten all this until after mum's death in 2002. The circumstances surrounding my discovery of the details were remarkable and in some way providential. For the last twelve years of her life my mum lived at St Peter's, the wonderful residence run by the Little Sisters of the Poor near the Oval in south London. When she first arrived she became involved in the life of the home, acting as secretary at committee meetings and taking part in the daily spiritual and social timetable, but as the years passed she came to suffer from a level of dementia, which made it impossible for her to carry on a coherent conversation for any length of time. Happily she never reached the stage of not recognising my sister and me, and since I was often in London I was able to visit her frequently. She also struggled with osteoporosis and eventually the almost inevitable happened and she broke her hip. The operation at nearby St Thomas' Hospital was a success, but she never managed to get mobile again and after a few weeks pneumonia took its toll. Fortunately that year I had not taken much holiday during the summer, so as mum's condition deteriorated in the late autumn I took two weeks off and went to stay at our house in Clapham. Towards the end of that fortnight mum was discharged by St Thomas' and returned to St Peter's and I accompanied her in the ambulance. It was a painful journey, watching her curled up like a little child, frightened and clinging to her beloved teddy bear. She cried out in pain each time the rather ancient vehicle hit a bump in the road, but eventually we arrived and settled her back into her room. The sisters, as always, were wonderful and my sister and I will be eternally grateful for their loving care over so many years.

The day after the trauma of mum's return home I felt in need of some time to myself and had decided to play a few holes of golf in spite of the unpromising weather forecast. I drove to Wimbledon Common but as the menacing clouds mounted I thought better of it and returned the car to the monastery garden in Clapham before heading up to town on the bus. By the time I reached Oxford Circus the heavens had opened and the rain was bouncing off the ground. The only recourse was to take shelter, but I did not feel like roaming round the shops after all, so I made my way to All Souls', Langham Place, the church outside the BBC's Broadcasting House at the top of Regent Street, but even the short walk from the bus to the church had left me soaked. I sat quietly at the back of the church trying to dry out and had not been there more than about five minutes when my mobile phone rang. Since I was alone in the church I had no qualms about answering it and it was the sisters, suggesting that I should come as soon as possible. I duly dashed to the Underground and was at my mum's bedside within the half-hour. She had in fact rallied by the time I arrived, but I called my sister in Birmingham and told her the situation. That was on the Friday and throughout the weekend we kept vigil with mum until she died peacefully on the Monday morning.

When the funeral was over my sister and I boxed mum's few belongings and took them back to Hampshire, so that we could go through them at our leisure. Within a day or two I had begun to go through mum's papers and I stumbled across a baptismal certificate, which immediately caught my eye. Amazingly it was headed "All Souls', Langham Place" and contained the details of mum's baptism as an eighteen-year-old in 1931. I am not claiming I received some special revelation but just sharing the real consolation I felt as I reflected on the fact that I was sitting in the very place where she was baptised when I was summoned to her deathbed.[11] I put the certificate away safely but within a day or two I found myself wanting to go back and have another look. Mysteriously there was a nagging voice inside me saying: "You did not take note of the date." When a few days later this happened for the third or fourth time I went back and found the certificate and to my amazement saw that the date of mum's baptism was 22nd November, the very day I had sat in the church seventy-one years later. Once again I assure you I am not reading anything more into this than the simple and consoling fact that all this led me to be more grateful than ever for the faith and the love of both my parents. I pondered again on the fact that my mother had come to faith as a young woman and seemingly without much encouragement from her own parents, and it was that faith in the abiding love of Jesus that she treasured and shared with me, above all by the life she lived and the sacrifices she made for the family.

There is just one addendum to this story. When I told my sister what had happened she shared with me something I had never known before. You need to know that my mother and my sister were great pals and great supports to one another. Mum had confided in Anne that before I was conceived she had been told that she might not be able to have any more children. Her response was to pray earnestly for a son and in particular that if the prayer was answered that he would become a priest. It was typical of her that she never shared this with me because both she and my father had made it clear that they did not want me to be under any external pressure with regard to my vocation. There was to be no question of my going ahead to fulfil their wishes. I recall them assuring me as I was leaving home that I would always be welcome back if it did not work out.

---

11 Mum was conditionally baptised at St Etheldreda's when she was received into full communion with the Catholic Church, but today that would not have happened. One of the great fruits of our entering into the ecumenical dialogue was the acceptance of our common baptism into the one Christian Church, so the ceremony at All Souls' was indeed the day of mum's baptism.

So where does all this lead us? It leads us to my point of departure at the beginning of a retreat. I treasure those moments of insight that come when we see connections in our lives and I invite you to begin thinking about your own lives and those moments when you can recognise that the hand of God was at work. I am conscious that if I were more attentive to the Lord I would probably see many more connections, so together we are going to explore what spiritual writers describe as the practice of the presence of God. We are not going in search of the extraordinary, but the ordinary. We are simply going to seek a growing awareness of our relationship with God, above all by exploring and meditating on the scriptures. We will endeavour to understand what St John means when he tells us that we are already the children of God (1 John 3:2) and St Paul when he points out that we are temples of the Holy Spirit (1 Corinthians 6:19; 2 Corinthians 6:16). We will try to grasp the fact that already we are living the new life that Jesus won for us at the resurrection (1 Corinthians 15:17-18) and that we are already caught up in a life of prayer by virtue of the fact that the Spirit of God is within us (Romans 8:26-27).

My hope is that together, and in spite of the troubles that continually beset us, we will become more and more grateful for what we have, able to stand in awe before the mystery of God and know that we are loved and redeemed.

Chapter Four
The power of God's word

The Emmaus story

It will be clear by now that the summer of 1989 broke the mould of my life and gave me a fresh start. The Christian Spirituality Summer School at Creighton University and particularly that scripture course from Marty Palmer provided me with what I can only describe as my Emmaus experience. It was the time when my heart was burning within me as he explained the scriptures to us.

As with so many passages in the scriptures, the Emmaus story encapsulates so much and invites us to make multiple connections. Recently the celebrated spiritual writer and speaker Ronald Rolheiser OMI gave me an unusual insight into the story when he dwelt on the fact that the disciples were heading away from Jerusalem to a place where, as it were, they could drown their sorrows. While today no one knows exactly where Emmaus is, he suggested that for those disciples it was the equivalent of Las Vegas. They were coming to terms with the fact that, after all, Jesus would not be the fulfilment of their dreams and they were in search of some distractions by way of compensation. The fact that they were stopped in their tracks and turned back is therefore immensely significant. The fact that they did not instantly recognise Jesus is also significant. How often have we missed his presence, missed the promptings of his Spirit because we were too preoccupied or too downcast to notice? And how often when we are down do we seek compensation in our lives by indulging ourselves in unhealthy ways? The key to it all is that Jesus began to make the connections for them:

> "You foolish men! So slow to believe the full message of the prophets! Was it not ordained that the Christ should suffer and so enter into his glory?" Then, starting with Moses and going through all the prophets, he explained to them the passages throughout the scriptures that were about himself. (Luke 24:25-27)

Bathed in the word of God

Our task is to follow the example of those disciples, to be obedient to the voice of the Father and listen to his Son, the Chosen One (Luke 9:35), and so come to an understanding of the mystery of ourselves and the world around us. But it is not just a matter of understanding, for there will always be a limit to our understanding. It has more to do with our attitude and our openness, our desire as it were to be immersed in God, our creator and redeemer. Timothy Radcliffe OP, when he was Master General of the Dominicans, wrote a letter to his Dominican family, which was later published in the *Religious Life Review,* and on this subject he wrote persuasively. This is an extract from the section entitled "Community of the Word":

> When a child is born, its parents immediately begin to talk to it. Long before it can understand, a child is fed with words, bathed and soothed with words. The mother and father do not talk to their child so as to communicate information. They are talking it into life. It becomes human in this sea of language. Slowly it will be able to find a place in the love that its parents share. It grows into a life that is human.
>
> So too we are transformed by immersion in the Word of God, addressed to us. We do not read the Word so as to seek information. We ponder it, study it, meditate on it, live with it, eat and drink it. "These words which I command you this day shall be upon your heart; and you shall teach them diligently to your children, and shall talk of them when you sit in your house, and when you walk by the way, and when you lie down, and when you rise" (Deuteronomy 6:6f). This word of God works in us, making us human, bringing us to life, forming us too in that friendship which is the very life of God…
>
> As the child is fed by the words of its parents, then it makes the liberating and terrifying discovery that it is not the centre of the world. Behind the breast there is a mother. Everything is not at its command. It discovers itself as part of the human community. In the conversation of our parents, we discover a world in which we may belong. So, too, as we are nourished by the word of God, we are led into a larger world. The good shepherd, who has come that we

may have life and have it more abundantly, is the one who opens the gate, so that we may come out and find large open spaces.[1]

I wish to interject a word of gratitude to authors like Radcliffe and Rolheiser, because I think it is so refreshing to have people like them who write in a language that touches the experience and mentality of the men and women of our age. When I set out on my religious journey with the Redemptorists so much of the spiritual and ascetical reading to which we were directed was remote and incomprehensible. I think I dealt with it for the most part by suspending judgement, but it meant that, as with much of the theology we studied, wonderful opportunities of growth were missed and we lived a kind of spiritual turmoil, convinced that we were hopelessly inadequate but convinced also that those who reached sanctity or who wrote about the spiritual life had moved onto another plane, which was largely inaccessible to ordinary mortals. My hope is that this book will invite you to realise with the Second Vatican Council that there is a universal call to holiness, which is accessible to all (see chapter V of *Lumen Gentium*, the Dogmatic Constitution on the Church[2]). Of course on this matter as on so much else the Council was recovering what the Church had always believed and taught. Indeed back in the seventeenth century St Francis de Sales wrote powerfully about the absurdity of trying to impose one kind of spirituality on everyone:

> Devotion must be exercised in different ways by the gentleman, the worker, the servant, the prince, the widow, the young girl, and the married woman. Not only is this true, but the practice of devotion must also be adapted to the strength, activities, and duties of each particular person... It is an error, or rather a heresy, to wish to banish the devout life from the regiment of soldiers, the mechanic's shop, the court of princes, or the home of married people... Purely contemplative, monastic, and religious devotion cannot be exercised in such states of life. However, besides those three kinds of devotion

---

1 Timothy Radcliffe OP, *The Promise of Life,* 25th February (Ash Wednesday) 1998, 3.1, "Community of the Word": < http://www.op.org/curia/MG/promise.htm> accessed 23rd February 2009.

2 In, for example, A. Flannery (ed.), *Vatican Council II: The Basic Sixteen Documents* (New York: Costello; Dublin: Dominican Publications, 1996).

there are several others adapted to bring perfection to those living in the secular state.[3]

I find the image of a child being bathed in words of love by its parents a beautiful metaphor for how the word of God, which is the ultimate word of love, can transform our lives. I would like to think that throughout these meditations on the word of God we will, as it were, be swimming in this sea of love. Indeed if we take Radcliffe's image back into the womb we know that even there the sound of the unborn child's parents' voices, especially of course its mother's, will be having its influence. How important, then, that the parents be at peace with one another and the world, for if they are not then their voices will convey their anger and frustration rather than the calm, contentment and joy of their love, and accordingly the child may be damaged.

The prayer of Paul

At the beginning of every lecture Marty Palmer prayed with us Paul's prayer in his letter to the Ephesians (3:14-21). This custom made such an impression on me that I have taken to doing the same before all my conferences and talks. Again it is one of those passages of scripture that are so rich in meaning and insight that it is easy to miss all that the author is saying and all the connections he is making. I say "author" at this point because scholars have raised doubts about the authorship of some of Paul's letters. Suffice it to say that I rather like the comment of Raymond Brown, the great scripture scholar, who in a lecture at the Franciscan Study Centre in Canterbury said that the authorship of the New Testament books was not something that preoccupied him. Putting everything into perspective, he said that if after his death books were attributed to him that he had not actually written, he was sure he would not mind! So we will leave it to others to pursue these matters and be satisfied that these books are in the canon of scripture and therefore are the word of God. These are the words of Paul's prayer:

---

3 St Francis de Sales, *Introduction to the Devout Life,* translated and edited by John K. Ryan (London: Doubleday, 1989), pp. 43, 44.

This, then, is what I pray, kneeling before the Father, from whom every family, whether spiritual or natural, takes its name:

Out of his infinite glory, may he give you the power through his Spirit for your hidden self to grow strong, so that Christ may live in your hearts through faith, and then, planted in love and built on love, you will with all the saints have strength to grasp the breadth and the length, the height and the depth; until, knowing the love of Christ, which is beyond all knowledge, you are filled with the utter fullness of God.

Glory be to him whose power, working in us, can do infinitely more than we can ask or imagine; glory be to him from generation to generation in the Church and in Christ Jesus for ever and ever. Amen.

At the heart of this prayer is the petition that our hidden self may grow strong – something that is brought about by the power of the Holy Spirit. To reach the innermost part of our being we need if possible to take time away, which is why retreats and times of recollection are so important and can be so valuable. Jesus gave us a wonderful example of this. On many occasions in the Gospels we are told that he withdrew to pray alone, sometimes even spending the night in prayer, for example the night before he chose the Twelve (see Luke 6:12). When we are called upon to discern before making key decisions in our lives it is important to follow this example and enter into our inner being in quiet and solitude. And even if it is impossible to take substantial time away we can still make space in our everyday lives. Jesus told us to go into our rooms and shut the door and pray to our Father (Matthew 6:6). The room here is to be interpreted not as our own private room in the house – we may not have one – but precisely the hidden self or inner part of our being that we have just identified. The Jesuits, who build their retreat work around the Spiritual Exercises of their founder, St Ignatius Loyola, have made provision for this in what they call the Nineteenth Annotation: the practice of the Spiritual Exercises in the midst of everyday life.

The discipline of prayer

The ideal to which we aspire is that of sanctifying every waking and sleeping moment, but the early hermits and monks realised that the human condition is such that we need the discipline of prayer times so that we can consciously consecrate ourselves and all that we are and do to God. The remarkable success of the BBC television series *The Monastery* illustrated just how effective it can be to withdraw and be immersed in a situation where each day is enshrined in prayer.[4] The monks at Worth Abbey welcomed five very modern men for forty days and forty nights and the television cameras tracked their progress as they shared in a timetable that called them to the abbey church six times a day. In due course each of them would give witness to the fact that those forty days had profoundly affected them. The monks follow the ancient Rule of St Benedict, which dates back fifteen hundred years and has stood the test of time, and in a book that resulted from the series Abbot Christopher Jamison has provided valuable pointers as to how we can apply the wisdom of the monastery to the busy world outside.[5]

Freedom

Prayer can be hard work, it does require commitment and effort, but, as we shall see when we deal explicitly with prayer in a later chapter, neither is it primarily an exercise in concentration, nor does its success depend on our ability to remain focused. Again I can speak only from my own experience, but for years I found retreats a burden, something to be endured because they were required by my rule as a Redemptorist, and I have found this to be the case with others, particularly with the clergy and other men and women in religious congregations. So when I preach retreats today I stress at the very beginning that I want the participants to be free, to go where the Spirit blows (John 3:8) – in modern parlance, to go with the flow. I remind everyone that we will all have our own agendas and what is important is that we find the best way of entering into our inner being so that we can reflect upon our stories, discover the truth about ourselves and about God, and so see more clearly how our stories are part of God's story. Jesus told us that the truth would set us free (John 8:32). It is clear from the context that this is the discovery of the truth about ourselves, including the painful truth that leads us to realise what may be holding us back and preventing us from living life to the full (John 10:10), including the sin that enslaves us.

---

4 This was a four-part BBC television documentary, filmed at Worth Abbey, West Sussex, in 2005.

5 C. Jamison, *Finding Sanctuary: Monastic Steps for Everyday Life* (London: Weidenfeld & Nicolson, 2006).

So we are back to the meditation that begins with our own stories and seeks to recognise the presence of God, already in the story. I think the way the Church invites us to use the Rite of Christian Initiation of Adults illustrates the method we should use. No longer is preparation for reception into full communion with the Catholic Church simply about adult catechesis. It has much more to do with enabling people to recognise the movement of the Spirit in their own lives: the Spirit who has prompted them over the years and brought them this far.

Mark's Gospel

I propose that the best possible starting point in the scriptures for this meditation is the Gospel of Mark. Mark's is one of the two basic sources for all the Synoptic Gospels (Matthew, Mark and Luke).[6] It is the shortest Gospel and has no infancy narrative. Throughout there is a sense of urgency: Mark is constantly telling us that things happened "at once". While it is the least systematic of the Synoptics, it sets out to show that despite the fact that Jesus was eventually rejected by the people, he was God's triumphant messenger, coming to the resurrection only through the pain and suffering of his passion and death.

It is particularly significant that the original text of Mark's Gospel ended at verse 8 of chapter 16. The women had gone to the tomb and been told to go to Peter and tell him that Jesus would meet the disciples in Galilee. However, Mark ends by telling us that the women "came out and ran away from the tomb because they were frightened out of their wits; and they said nothing to a soul, for they were afraid…" Shorter and longer endings were subsequently added to round off the Gospel and bring it in line with what the other evangelists say, but by staying with this abrupt and rather alarming ending, we are provided with a perfect springboard for a time of retreat. The Gospel did not come to a neat and tidy end, but it is being lived out by you and me in our world today. There is confusion and fear in our lives as there was in the lives of those faithful women. It is for us to complete the Gospel story with our stories. We are as it were continuing to write the Gospel. Like Mary, we are to hear the word of God and obey it (Luke 11:27-28).

---

6 These three Gospels are so alike that it is possible to place the corresponding passages side by side and see them at a glance: hence the use of the word synoptic, "with one eye".

Chapter Five
Making the connections

The jigsaw puzzle of life

I have already made much of the value of being able to see and make connections. One of my favourite analogies is the jigsaw puzzle. Thankfully most of us can look back on times in our lives when everything was going smoothly. The various dimensions were fitting into place and we found ourselves at one with the world around us. It was as if the pieces of the jigsaw puzzle had fallen into place and we could see a picture clearly emerging: a picture of where we were going and how we were being fulfilled. Sadly, for many those times are all too fleeting and a more fitting image would be of a jigsaw with most of the pieces scattered and very little of the picture clear. Indeed when some crisis arises it is almost as if something or someone has deliberately turned the table over and left the jigsaw in disarray and we are left to begin all over again, trying to piece it together. I think times of retreat or mission provide opportunities for people metaphorically to work on the jigsaw of their lives, and there is no better place to begin than by looking at the bigger picture revealed in the scriptures of the Old and New Testaments.

Jesus and his disciples

When Jesus is teaching his disciples, we often see them being slow to grasp the message and piece the jigsaw together. Jesus remains untiringly patient with them, sometimes coaxing them, sometimes upbraiding them, sometimes suggesting they withdraw and rest awhile. Peter is always being presented to us as the prime example of someone who is full of goodwill, desperate to please and get it right, but who continually puts his foot in it. He is like the child in class who always shoots their hand up when a question is asked but who so often gets the answer wrong. Is it not ironic that almost immediately after Peter's great declaration of faith, "You are the Christ", Jesus rounds on him and says: "Get behind me, Satan!" (Matthew 16:13-23; Mark 8:27-33)? The reason for Jesus' dramatic reaction is that he knows he must go up to Jerusalem and fulfil his destiny and Peter understandably is fearful of the consequences.

The transfiguration

It is no coincidence therefore that soon after these events Jesus takes Peter as well as James and John up the mountain and they experience his transfiguration. This was an event of immense significance. It is recorded in each of the Synoptic Gospels and Peter refers to it in his second letter.[1] Again Peter seems at a loss to know what to say or do, but he recognises that something remarkable is happening and that they are wonderfully privileged to be present; and it seems that he does not want the moment to pass, suggesting that they build tents for Jesus and his visitors, Moses and Elijah. Both Mark and Matthew record that when they come down from the mountain Jesus gives them orders not to tell anyone about what has happened until after his resurrection.

Here is a perfect illustration of a scripture passage that can only be understood when it is pieced together with the rest of the story. Jesus knew that the disciples who accompanied him up the mountain would not be able to comprehend the meaning of what had taken place until they had more of the pieces of the story in place, and even after the resurrection it would seem that it took them time before everything did fall into place. Indeed Peter, who after they had gone up to Jerusalem assured Jesus of his undying loyalty, was to fulfil Jesus' prediction that he would deny knowing him three times. Peter's abject misery at those betrayals touches our hearts, but on Easter morning we see him running to the tomb when the news broke that the women had found it empty.

Fascinatingly, even after Jesus has appeared to the disciples on two different occasions in the upper room, it seems as though Peter and his companions have returned to their former trade as fishermen and are not clear that anything more will be required of them; but then Jesus comes and has breakfast with them on the shore. Peter is again centre stage as first he jumps into the water when he realises that it is Jesus who is issuing instructions, and then there follows a moving exchange as Jesus asks him three times whether he truly loves him. As Peter professes his love each time, we are told that the third time he is hurt and says to Jesus: "Lord, you know everything; you know I love you" (John 21:17). And so the three denials are forgiven, Peter is healed and, just as when they first met, Jesus again calls him to follow him. Everything is carefully and beautifully crafted in the Gospels: make no mistake about

---

1 Matthew 17:1-8; Mark 9:2-8; Luke 9:28-36; 2 Peter 1:16-18.

it. It is presented so that you and I will see the connections and become disciples ourselves.

Before we move on I would like to offer a further thought about the transfiguration. Clearly this was a powerful moment in Jesus' life on earth, in which the Father assured him that he enjoyed his favour. It was a moment designed to sustain Jesus and those favoured disciples through the pain and confusion of his passion and death, and its full import would only be grasped and shared when Jesus entered into his glory. It seems to me that we all need moments of transfiguration during our lives to sustain us. I think it is good to look back and try to identify transfiguring moments, when we have been as it were lifted out of ourselves and caught a glimpse of God. Go back to those moments, especially in times of difficulty or despondency. They may well sustain you during the troubled times and enable you to cope.

I recall one such powerful experience and it was actually on Mount Tabor, traditionally thought to be the mountain of the transfiguration. Only once have I visited the Holy Land and it was in the autumn of 1989. A thoughtful confrère, Father Tony Hodgetts, was leading a pilgrimage from his parish in Liverpool and asked me if I would like to join them. This was in the wake of that difficult period in my life when I had left Sunderland and I was still feeling a little fragile and prone to the odd panic attack. In the event it was one of the most wonderful weeks of my life. The weather was perfect and it was a joy to walk the same ground that Jesus had walked two thousand years ago. On the day we visited Mount Tabor, Tony asked me if I would like to lead the Eucharist. Hesitantly I agreed. We celebrated the Mass of the Transfiguration and I will always remember the extraordinary calm that came over me. The memory sustains me to this day.

We will never exhaust the treasure that we have in the scriptures and the richness of each passage. All I can hope is that in these pages I can help whet your appetite so that you will want to know more and search for your own connections. At every stage the evangelists are offering us pointers and again in the story of the transfiguration it would be a pity to miss the significance of Moses and Elijah. Moses represents the Law and Elijah the Prophets and you will recall that Jesus had come to bring both of these to fulfilment: "Do not imagine that I have come to abolish the Law or the Prophets. I have come not to abolish but to complete them" (Matthew 5:17).

Nurturing our spirits within the community

One of Marty Palmer's strategies was to return occasionally to Paul's prayer in Ephesians (3:14-21) and highlight elements that even after its daily use we might so easily have missed. It was something that appealed to me and I will share a few of those insights now. By way of continuing to nurture your own prayerful reading of the word of God, I suggest that you too might return to this prayer from time to time, for in many ways it is a wonderful summary of the whole Christian life.

For example, so far in this book we have been focusing largely on the personal side of our spiritual lives: the part that is concerned with the strengthening of our inner being. In Ephesians Paul prays that "Christ may live in your hearts through faith", and then moves on to pray about love: "planted in love and built on love, you will with all the saints have strength to grasp the breadth and the length, the height and the depth; until, knowing the love of Christ, which is beyond all knowledge, you are filled with the utter fullness of God". Palmer homed in on the juxtaposition of the words "planted" and "built".[2] Our love is to be like a plant with deep roots, which allow us to grow and blossom; and it is to be like a solid structure, built on firm foundations. There is a wealth of material to contemplate here and already we see connections with Jesus and his teaching. We can mature, develop and bear much fruit only when we are attached to the true vine, Jesus himself (John 15:1-8). The foolish person builds a house on sand, which will disintegrate in the storm; the wise person builds on solid rock, which can withstand whatever buffetings it receives (Matthew 7:24-27).

At the same time, it is also important when looking for the connections, not to concentrate solely on ourselves and our personal relationship with the Lord, but to remember that always we are part of a community of faith. So it is worth noting that Paul begins his prayer, "This, then, is what I pray, kneeling before the Father, from whom every family, whether spiritual or natural, takes its name", and of course we do not come to know the mystery of God's love by ourselves but in the company of "all the saints". We are all part of God's family, those of us who are living now and those who have gone before us, hopefully having already taken their places in heaven. In his letter to the Romans Paul puts it like this:

---

2 The juxtaposition of ideas is a literary device used in both the Old and New Testaments: just think of the wonderful way in which the two creation stories complement one another at the beginning of Genesis.

The life and death of each of us has its influence on others; if we live, we live for the Lord; and if we die, we die for the Lord, so that alive or dead we belong to the Lord. This explains why Christ both died and came to life, it was so that he might be Lord both of the dead and of the living. (14:7-9)

This text is often used at funerals. It leads us to gratitude for what we have received from others. By the same token it also reminds us of the serious responsibility we carry to give good example, to be signs of Christ's presence for one another.

So there is always this interconnectedness. We cannot get away from it. Not even hermits can get away from it. Remember, we are not isolated individuals, struggling to cope with life and searching for God alone. We are all part of God's family, created for God and for one another.

The New Testament is the fulfilment of the Old

The New Testament authors go to enormous lengths to ensure that we see the connections at every turn. How often are we reminded that this was what the prophets foretold? How often do we find Jesus directly quoting the prophets' words? And where it is not so explicit, those who know their Old Testament – and among them would have been all the converts from Judaism in the early Church – will be quick to see the connections. For example, when Jesus is being tempted in the wilderness, he responds to each temptation by quoting directly from the book of Deuteronomy (see Matthew 4:1-11).

The full text of the *Jerusalem Bible* is particularly helpful, providing us throughout with all the cross references, making sure those of us who need prompting do not miss any of the connections. There is no doubt that the New Testament authors went out of their way to construct the message so that we could see that Jesus was indeed the expected Messiah, but that should in no way weaken the power of what they have to say: rather it highlights the meticulous care they took in presenting the Good News. In the Bible we have the treasure of God's word and also some of the most brilliant and enduring literature that has ever been written.

In determining the books that make up the scriptures, the Church, as well as acknowledging their literary importance, is assuring us that they are the inspired word of God: that these are the books that God wants us to have so that we can enter into the mystery of our salvation. At the same time it should be clear to us that not all the books are of equal importance: indeed there are a few that are disputed and do not appear in the canons of all the Christian traditions, and these are known as the apocryphal or deuterocanonical books. Certainly I would not advise anyone to follow my example as a youngster of ploughing through the whole of the scriptures from the first sentence of Genesis to the last of the Apocalypse in the fond belief that the Redemptorists would have expected me to have read the whole of the Bible before going to the novitiate. Much of the time I had little idea of what it was all about and no idea of how it related to me and my life. For that reason I was delighted in recent times to have had the opportunity to republish a superb little book by Father John Daley called *Getting to Know the Bible*.[3] John is a Rosminian who originally designed this excellent introduction to the scriptures for his own parishioners. The intention was that, over the course of a year, they would have a basic understanding of the make-up of the Bible and some awareness of how it knits together as a whole. He does not begin with the book of Genesis but with Matthew's Gospel, and thereby indicates that he is going to help us see the connections right from the beginning. Then he cleverly introduces individual books or sets of books, intermingling those from the Old and New Testaments, so that gradually we see them all as part of one great tapestry. By situating the different books or groups of books in their literary genres and historical contexts, he immediately provides the reader with starting points for understanding and interpreting their messages.

Ultimately we are striving to attain that level of understanding which helps us to value the Bible as providing us with all that we need for our salvation. John concludes his Gospel by explaining this very succinctly. In the final sentences, referring to himself as "the disciple Jesus loved", he establishes his authority and then adds a touch of hyperbole:

> This disciple is the one who vouches for these things and has written them down, and we know that his testimony is true.
> There are many other things that Jesus did; if all were written down, the world itself, I suppose, would not hold all the books that would have to be written. (John 21:24-25)

---

3 Chawton: Redemptorist Publications, 2005.

I suggest that even more telling is the way he concludes his previous chapter:

> There were many other signs that Jesus worked and the disciples saw, but they are not recorded in this book. These are recorded so that you may believe that Jesus is the Christ, the Son of God, and that believing this you may have life through his name. (John 20:30-31)

So there we have it. The scriptures are more than an interesting collection of ancient books, which tell a remarkable story. They are the inspired word of God, offered to us that we might come to know Jesus and live the life he won for us. As the remaining chapters of this book unfold, that will be our sole concern: to reflect on the word of God, so that it may come alive for us and enable us to live this life to the full (see John 10:10).

It is worth remembering that each of the books was written at a particular time for a particular community. Therefore they are written with specific agendas and each has a particular community and its needs in mind. This is well illustrated by the New Testament letters. When Paul writes to the Christians in Corinth he is conscious of the constant threats to their faith, living in a port that is not just a magnet for people with all kinds of other religious affiliations but also a notorious centre for immoral behaviour. By contrast when he is writing to the Galatians and the Romans he is more concerned with how Christianity relates to Judaism. The disciples who had accompanied Jesus had remained faithful to many of the Jewish traditions, but now the question arose of to what extent these should be imposed on the Gentile converts. These problems were finally resolved at the first council held in Jerusalem (see Acts 15 and Galatians 2). It is also fascinating to note how someone like Paul had his understanding shaped by the passage of time. His first letters were to the Thessalonians and it is clear that in those early days he fully expected the second coming of Jesus at any time and wrote accordingly, assuring them that when the time came those who had died would have no advantage over those who were still alive (see 1 Thessalonians 4:15-17). In the later letters there is no such emphasis though there remains a sense of urgency and the clear call to live in the present and deal with the issues of the day in the light of the Gospel.

Even as a youngster, one of the most enriching and indeed liberating discoveries for me was the realisation that generally, when I was reading the scriptures, I was not reading eyewitness accounts of events such as the media offer us about our world today. This was not breaking news. This was news that had been handed on by word of mouth for decades, and in the case of some of the Old Testament books for generations, before it was put down in writing. It was the distilled version of events, presented so that we would be able to grasp not just the facts but the meaning of the facts. I recall our own Redemptorist scholar Denis McBride reminding us that in the infancy narratives in Luke's Gospel, the angels are dancing in the sky and singing, "Glory to God in the highest heaven", so that we can recognise that the little child, born in poverty in a stable in Bethlehem, is in fact the saviour of the world. When you go back to the creation stories in Genesis you can marvel at the extraordinarily sophisticated insights of the authors as long as you are not reading them as literal accounts of what happened. This is why "creationism", which seems to be capturing the imagination of some fundamentalist groups on both sides of the Atlantic, is such a tragedy. Far from leading us to a faithful following of Christ, it impoverishes the message and sells us short.

In this respect often I have felt saddened after a visit from Jehovah's Witnesses. Knowing the challenge of roaming the streets and knocking on doors, I admire their zeal. They are surely good and committed people, but their attempts at evangelisation seem limited to trading scripture quotations. They give the impression that they believe the scriptures somehow fell from heaven. They seem to me to have little or no consciousness that these testimonies emerged from communities of faith, which, as we have already noted, even wrestled over which books to include in their canons.

In a similar vein I will always remember a discussion with some prisoners after Mass one Sunday morning in Canterbury. I had been supplying at the prison for some weeks and had got to know the group quite well. They were not all Catholics, but they came each week with great reverence and devotion and they certainly listened attentively to the homilies. Indeed, a small group would usually engage me over a cup of coffee afterwards and on this particular Sunday for one of them my homily had obviously been too much to stomach. I honestly cannot remember what the issues were, but I do recall his parting shot: "Father, you will never convince me: I am a rib man myself." I could only agree to disagree.

Of course the story of God taking a rib from Adam to form Eve is one of the most beautiful stories in the Old Testament. It is part of the second creation story (see Genesis 2:5-25) and reveals much to us about our relationships, not only with God but with one another. In chapter one of Genesis we are told that God created us male and female and put us in charge of the earth, but complementing that story comes the second story. Now we are shown to be vulnerable and very much in need of love and companionship: a further reminder of just how much we need one another. We noted above how Paul juxtaposes the notions of our being planted and built on love: here at the beginning of Genesis with the two creation stories is another wonderful example of the juxtaposition of ideas in the scriptures, enabling us to grow in awareness and understanding of God's plan.

Chapter Six
In the beginning

Reading the scriptures in the light of your own experience

During that remarkable scripture foundation course with Marty Palmer, I will always remember that after telling us to read the New Testament twice, the next exercise he invited us to undertake was also challenging and rewarding. You may wish to find the time to try it as well. He suggested that we read the first eleven chapters of Genesis, not as an ancient story, describing creation and the origins and early experiences of humankind, but rather as a description of the world as we know it. For me it proved to be stunningly helpful. There indeed was a description that matched exactly how I experience my own struggles and those of my fellow men and women, measuring the beauty, wonder and potential that are not only around us but in us, against the tragedy, pain and suffering that see so many of our dreams shattered or unfulfilled. If in the future someone should ask you to explain the problem of suffering and evil, take them back to those chapters of Genesis and invite them to read with an open mind. In those pages there is no attempt to construct a philosophical argument nor is there any shying away from the reality. As we say today: the reality is named and explained.

If our starting point in understanding the authors of the scriptures is that they were people like ourselves, searching for meaning, struggling with their humanity and the vagaries of life in their own times and places, we will be well placed to enter deeply into the mystery of the realities about which they wrote, and to translate their message as something relevant to our own experiences and struggles.

Creation

Let us for a moment return to the creation stories in Genesis and see again how we are provided with beautiful and searching insights into the wonder and goodness of ourselves and the world around us. They also point to what constitutes our right relationship with God, the creator, and, flowing from that, right and healthy relationships with one another. The second creation story concludes with the reminder that the man "leaves his father and his mother and joins himself to his wife, and they become one body" (Genesis 2:24). Take note of this oneness at the very beginning. It is central to our reflections throughout this book. So at the end of chapter two of Genesis we might say that everything is rosy in the garden. God has completed the work of creation. Everything has its place: there is a beautiful symmetry and order to everything – but that order is not to last.

Probably the greatest stumbling blocks to faith are the problems of evil and suffering. How often are we as Christians asked: how could a good and loving God allow certain things to happen? We may sometimes respond by pointing out that the evil is the direct result of human beings choosing to be selfish, proud, brutal and loveless, but there remains the problem of natural tragedies for which it is not clear that anyone can be held responsible. Of course, today there is a growing sense that certain natural disasters may be at least in part the result of global warming, and this should challenge us to accept our corporate responsibility for what is going on and ask whether we can justify the cost of maintaining selfish lifestyles which deprive others of their basic human rights. As the global economy expands and we rapidly use up many known natural resources, the future does look somewhat bleak, though the urgency of the situation does seem to be dawning and in spite of all the vested interests of the strong and wealthy – both nations and individuals – it may be that ultimately the doomsday scenario will concentrate minds across the globe to work together to avoid catastrophe.

Interestingly, if that happens it will in a sense still be a selfish response: albeit the natural response of self-preservation. I recall an eminent geologist reminding a conference which I was attending that, while we glibly speak about saving the planet, we are really speaking about saving ourselves. He astutely pointed out that no matter what we do to the planet, it will ultimately right the balance itself, as it has always done over the billions of years of its existence, whether we survive to witness it or not!

It is not that I want to dismiss this subject as too complicated, but I am not going to spend time wrestling with it further. Suffice it to say that I am convinced that we are called to live in harmony with one another and with the whole of creation. I believe that what is happening now provides us as Christians with wonderful opportunities to examine our consciences about our lifestyles and how we respond to Christ's invitation to live simply with a constant concern for others.[1] It is to the scriptures that I wish to turn continually so that our meditation on all these matters may be informed by the word of God. And since Genesis is given its name because it deals with the beginning of things, we will stay with Genesis for a while.

The Fall

The story of the Fall is not so much an account of disobedience but of how human beings try to grab the good things of God's world for themselves. The temptation is not precisely about the eating of a piece of forbidden fruit but rather about taking over God's world and being in control. When the woman is hesitant about falling for the temptation, the serpent says to her: "You will not die! God knows in fact that on the day you eat it your eyes will be opened and you will be like gods" (Genesis 3:4-5). Therein is the real temptation: we want to play God – to be in control. The consequence of such behaviour is that everything immediately becomes disordered: our relationship with God; our relationships with each other.

And so the story unfolds. Our first parents are quick to feel a sense of shame and in no time the problems begin to mount. Their children are at odds and jealousy leads to murder as Cain disposes of Abel (4:8). Revenge is the order of the day for Lamech, who takes violence to an altogether new level (4:24). God is described as having a grieving heart and regretting ever having created humankind, and so comes the purging with the flood (chapters 6–8). Noah is described as a man of integrity and accordingly a fresh start is made with him, but his descendants also begin to rely on their own strength and seek to control things as they try to bridge the gap between heaven and earth with their famous tower. The Tower of Babel perfectly symbolises the breakdown of relationships which we see all around us. We fail to understand one another's languages. Bear in mind that it is not just the spoken words we may not understand but equally the gestures and behaviour of those around us.

---

1 CAFOD (Catholic Agency for Overseas Development) has initiated a wonderful campaign called *livesimply,* providing really practical ways in which we can deal with the rampant consumerism that surrounds us. It has captured the imagination of many in our parishes and schools.

The message is loud and clear: human beings have set themselves on a course of self-destruction and they are incapable of saving themselves.

Of course, in the story, God's intervention is described in human terms, but it is important to note that what happens is always a consequence of human behaviour. The consequences of the Fall are dramatic and considerable. No longer do human beings enjoy the favour of God and a peaceful and ordered existence in their habitat in the Garden of Eden.

Biblical thinking

Before proceeding it will be helpful to get some understanding of how the biblical writers understood life and death and salvation. The first point to note is that, in both Old and New Testaments, their understanding was very different from the Greek philosophical notions that subsequently dominated our theology and therefore the way so many of us were taught the catechism. For Aristotle, whose thinking had such an influence on theologians like St Thomas Aquinas (1225–74) and the scholastic school, God created all the different elements and creatures, and each had its own substance and accidents. In other words if you are speaking about a table, then its substance is the fact that it is a table and can be used as such; its accidents are things whereby you recognise it as this particular table: for example, the number of legs it has, its colour and so on. When you apply this theory to men and women, our substance is our humanity and the accidents are the things that make us distinctive and individual. God gave us our being and our life. Our relationship with God is religion, but religion too would come under the category of an accident.

By contrast, the biblical writers thought very differently. For them God is being and our being – our existence – is a share in God's being. And so we only exist by virtue of our relationship with God, like a ray of light from a lamp. We are not like tables that are made and can be shipped off. From Genesis to the Apocalypse this is the philosophy that holds good. It is essential that we know this if we are to understand that in the biblical vision the very substance of our life and being is communion with God and one another.

Theoretically, then, humanity should no longer have existed after the Fall, bearing in mind that the biblical notion of life is that all being is rooted in God and human life is a share in God's being. Since humanity has rejected God it has rejected the source of life. The Old Testament writers struggle with this. They see us living a sort of half-life, rather like a flower that has been uprooted and put in a vase. We remain alive but only partially and, when we die, we exist no more. That is why they so often plead with God for an extension of life. The psalmist reminds the Lord: "From the grave, who can give you praise?" (Psalm 6:6).

The promise of a saviour

After all that has preceded it in the previous eleven chapters it is remarkable that the mood dramatically changes in chapter twelve of Genesis. Seemingly for no reason other than God's gracious goodness there is the promise to Abraham that a saviour will come. In a sense we could say that this is the beginning of the Gospel, the Good News that will unfold through the ups and downs of God's chosen people in the Old Testament until the promise is fulfilled in the most unlikely of circumstances: the birth of a little child in poverty in Bethlehem.

In spite of all those centuries of preparation for the coming, the advent, of the saviour, the people were not prepared. As they wrestled with their own problems and challenges they developed their own ideas about the God who created them. They remained prey to the temptation to go off and worship idols of their own making instead of the God who kept calling them back through the prophets: a temptation that besets us just as much even though our idols may not be golden calves or statues made of bronze. When reading the Old Testament we need to be patient with the people and with ourselves. Theirs was an understanding of the mystery of God, born of their limited knowledge and experience. Of course our understanding is also limited, but we have the rich treasure of the revelation in the New Testament that we have been reconciled to God in Christ (2 Corinthians 5:18).

Jesus challenges their preconceptions

Even with his apostles and close disciples Jesus had patiently to dismantle many of their preconceived ideas of the saviour or Messiah: effectively he had to turn their way of thinking upside down. Indeed we might even say that it was only gradually that Jesus himself came to realise that he had come not just for his own people but for all men and women of all time. When Jesus sends the Twelve on their first mission he specifically forbids them to work with those who are not their own: "Do not turn your steps to pagan territory, and do not enter any Samaritan town; go rather to the lost sheep of the House of Israel" (Matthew 10:5-6).

In chapter fifteen of Matthew's Gospel, in response to the pleas of the Canaanite woman on behalf of her daughter, Jesus again insists that he was sent only to the lost sheep of the House of Israel and even rebuffs her by saying, "It is not fair to take the children's food and throw it to the house-dogs." However, she gives as good as she gets and reminds Jesus that "even house-dogs can eat the scraps that fall from their master's table". Jesus seems deeply moved by this exchange: "Woman, you have great faith. Let your wish be granted" (15:24-28).

By the time John's Gospel is written at the end of the first century the fact that Jesus had come for all is interwoven from the outset: "Yes, God loved the world so much that he gave his only Son, so that everyone who believes in him may not be lost but may have eternal life" (3:16). And then we have the wonderful encounter with the Samaritan woman in chapter four, a story I will return to in a different context later in the book.

Be sure that all this took time: remember that the great dispute within the Church during the first century was about the extent to which Gentile converts should be subjected to Jewish customs, and it led to a showdown between Peter and Paul and the first council at Jerusalem (see Galatians 2; Acts 15). So do not be surprised if in our own day it takes time to resolve tensions within the family of the Church. As the psychologists and spiritual writers like to remind us, we are all shaped by our experiences and inevitably we all carry a lot of baggage from the past.

A kingdom for all

Initially the problem for the disciples was that they were clinging to the fundamental belief that the Messiah would ensure the triumph of their nation as God's chosen people. Some clearly thought that by following Jesus they would be entitled to some kind of preferment. Remember how James and John approached Jesus and asked him for places at his side in the kingdom, and how angry the others were when they found out (Mark 10:35-45). Fascinatingly Matthew has their mother asking on their behalf (20:20-21): was it that he feared his readers would have been too scandalised to think that the brothers could have asked for themselves? Jesus dealt with the request calmly and used the opportunity to move their mindset: "Can you drink the cup that I must drink, or be baptised with the baptism with which I must be baptised?" (Mark 10:38).

The challenge for them and for us is whether we are willing to accept the consequences of discipleship and follow Jesus by taking up the cross. When the disciples had been arguing about who was the greatest, Jesus had introduced them to his new, upside-down view of the world: "If anyone wants to be first, he must make himself last of all and servant of all" (Mark 9:35). This teaching is reinforced over and over again. In Matthew's Gospel when Jesus first speaks about taking up the cross he adds this further challenging paradox: "Anyone who finds his life will lose it; anyone who loses his life for my sake will find it" (10:39).

A kingdom of service

Of course the key to understanding all this is that Jesus' community is not one where those in authority lord it over the rest, but where everyone is at the service of the other (Mark 10:42-45); and this is the culmination of Jesus' teaching in John as he comes to the Last Supper and demonstrates what he means by washing the disciples' feet (13:1-17). Gerhard Lohfink develops this central theme of the Gospel story quite brilliantly in his book *Jesus and Community: The Social Dimension of Christian Faith*. I do not think that anyone would dispute that this is the consistent teaching of Jesus and that he demonstrated how to live in this way in his life and in his death, yet it remains an enormous challenge to each of us as individuals and to the church community as a whole to remain faithful. Power can be very seductive and it is easy to be convinced that we are exercising authority for the good of others by imposing on them our values and beliefs. Lohfink highlights the danger with this telling passage:

> It is one of the church's tragic blind spots that it again and again seeks to protect its authority (which is certainly necessary and legitimate) through *domination*. In reality it undermines its authority in this way and does serious harm to the gospel. True authority can

shine forth only in the weakness of renouncing domination. True authority is the authority of the Crucified. Paul knew this better than anyone else; for this reason he constantly connected the paradox of his apostolic authority with the paradox of the Crucified and Risen One. It is astonishing how intensely the substance of Mark 10:42-45 reappears in Paul.[2]

---

2 G. Lohfink, *Jesus and Community: The Social Dimension of Christian Faith,* translated by John P. Galvin (New York: Paulist Press, 1984), p.120.

Chapter Seven
Reverence for the word of God

When to genuflect

Ronald Rolheiser once wrote about the great emptiness that must exist for people who have nothing or no one before whom they feel moved to genuflect.[1] The Catholic tradition of genuflecting before the Blessed Sacrament is a constant reminder of the wondrous gift that is ours, the real presence of our Lord in the sacrament of the Eucharist. I feel sure it is a custom we do well to treasure and nurture. And we would also do well to remember that a similar reverence for the word of God in the scriptures is also part of our heritage. In the Tridentine rite the Last Gospel was part of every Eucharist: a reading of the Prologue of St John prior to the blessing and dismissal. When the priest reached the words, "And the Word was made flesh and dwelt among us", he and the congregation would genuflect. Incidentally we retain the custom in the new rite when we remember the incarnation during the creed on Christmas Day and on the feast of the Annunciation. Here are reminders of the presence of the Lord, touching and transforming our lives with the power of his word.

When the liturgy is celebrated with solemnity, great reverence is shown to the book of the Gospels: it is carried through the church in procession with candles and incense. And whenever the Gospel has been proclaimed in the assembly the priest or deacon reverently kisses the book.

Ezra the scribe

There is a wonderful story in the book of Nehemiah which tells us that Ezra, the scribe and priest, was told by the people to bring the book of the Law of Moses and read from it. He stood on a wooden platform

---

1   Ronald Rolheiser, Weekly Column, 6th January 2008: <http://www.ronrolheiser.com/columnarchive/archive_display.php?rec_id=389> accessed 23rd February 2009.

and read from early morning until midday. We are also told that when he opened the book all the people stood up and Ezra blessed the Lord, the great God, whereupon the people answered, "Amen! Amen!" Then they bowed their heads and worshipped the Lord with their faces to the ground (see Nehemiah 8).

If such was the reverence of the Old Testament people for the book, how much more should we stand in awe before the revelation that comes with Jesus and the New Testament: a testament that was sealed in his blood. In the letter to the Hebrews we are told that the word of God is alive and active and that it cuts more finely than any double-edged sword, able to judge the thoughts and intentions of our hearts (4:12). In his second letter to Timothy, Paul points out that "all scripture is inspired by God and can profitably be used for teaching, for refuting error, for guiding people's lives and teaching them to be holy" (3:16).

Using the scriptures

I have already indicated that one way of getting to know the Bible would be to follow a reading guide such as Father John Daley designed for his parishioners (see chapter five above). For those of us who are able to follow the liturgical cycle we are fed with a daily diet of readings from both the Old and New Testaments, but inevitably they come to us as snippets and sometimes large sections of particular books are left out. Nevertheless it is to be hoped that as we become permeated by the constant repetition of the message we will, as Timothy Radcliffe suggests, be bathed in the word. I suggest that this could be true especially of how the psalms, which form the backbone of the Divine Office or Prayer of the Church, affect us. We will return to the psalms when we consider our prayer lives more closely.

For the rest it is not my intention to try in any systematic way to work through the different books of the Bible. It is enough for us to realise that this rich treasure is our heritage and that the more familiar we become with it the more in touch we become with God's story, which in turn is our story. The trick of course is that not only do we get to know the story, but we get to know God and arrive at that point to which John, in his Gospel, is so concerned to bring us: "These [signs] are recorded so that you may believe that Jesus is the Christ, the Son of God, and that believing this you may have life through his name" (John 20:31).

The focus is always on Jesus

For the Christian the whole of the Bible is read in the light of Jesus and above all of his resurrection, and I shall be seeking to explain how vital it is that we never lose sight of this fact. There are those who are nonplussed by the image of the God of the Old Testament and cannot understand how anyone can seriously reverence many of the texts. But we read them in the knowledge that it was from these people, with all their faults and failings and in spite of all their struggles, that God chose to send his Son into our world. The mystery of the plan of salvation is precisely that it respected the freedom of the people God had created and that the saviour came into the mess, as one of us, and showed us a wholly new way of living and a wholly new understanding of God.

The Exodus

At the Easter Vigil, the great liturgical celebration of the year, we go back over the history of our salvation and at the heart of it is the story of the Exodus, when the people of Israel finally escaped from the oppression of their time in Egypt. Whatever readings might be left out on that night, the one Old Testament reading that is a must is from the book of Exodus. Pharaoh's chariots and horsemen are first clogged in the mud and then engulfed by the waters that had previously parted to let the Israelites cross. The reading ends: "It was then that Moses and the sons of Israel sang this song in honour of the Lord", and we sing the psalm that is the continuation of the Exodus reading.

To be perfectly honest I always find myself feeling more than a little uneasy as we cheer God for being a great warrior:

> The Lord is a warrior! The Lord is his name.
> The chariots of Pharaoh he hurled into the sea,
> the flower of his army is drowned in the sea.
> The deeps hide them; they sank like a stone.
>
> Your right hand, Lord, glorious in its power,
> your right hand, Lord, has shattered the enemy.
> In the greatness of your glory you crushed the foe. (Exodus 15:3-6)

Of course, only two nights previously, on Maundy Thursday, we also recall the Passover, another of the great events of salvation history, which had prepared the way for the Exodus (see Exodus 12). The people had been commanded to celebrate the final plague that had struck the Egyptians, namely the striking down of their firstborn. The meal was carefully prescribed and had to be eaten hastily in preparation for their departure, for this would be the event that would finally force Pharaoh to let them go – although he tried to renege on that and hence the drama of the Exodus.

How then do we relate to this God of the Old Testament, the God depicted in these stories, the God who is glorified for crushing Israel's enemies?

In the first place I believe we must return to the point that the people of Israel were interpreting their experience, making sense of all that was happening to them. The underlying message throughout the story of the Old Testament is that when the people behaved honourably to one another and gave God pride of place, then all went well and they ended up triumphant. By contrast when they tried to go it alone and disobeyed what they knew to be right they ended up in a mess. The message of the prophets is constant: they call the people back to a right way of living, a way of obedience to God's laws. In their dire warnings about the consequences of not being faithful we see them appealing to the people to reflect on their experiences to date.

It would be easy for us to take a superior position, but we know that Christians have often responded to their own ups and downs in similar fashion. If you look back to the reaction in Britain of the Christian churches after the two world wars of the last century you will see a similar interpretation of events. There were deeply held convictions among Christians in Britain that right was "on our side" and particularly that the triumph over Hitler was by the grace of God. Today we are learning to be more cautious and more discerning. Please do not misunderstand what I am saying. I am not trying to suggest that Hitler was anything other than a very evil man and that it was right to resist him, but we are now able to look back and ask questions about what is morally acceptable even in such a horrific conflict. And indeed when the war was over in Europe, to this day consciences are troubled by the suffering caused by the dropping of atomic bombs on Hiroshima and Nagasaki to bring it to an end in the Far East.

It was interesting to witness the furore there was in 1982 when the Thanksgiving Service at St Paul's Cathedral after the Falklands War included prayers for the people of Argentina and especially those who had fallen. It took until the Millennium celebrations in 2000 for a pope, John Paul II, to apologise to the Muslim community for the Crusades centuries before. But we should rejoice at these acts of reconciliation, which I believe are Gospel-centred. The Father whom Jesus revealed to us was not a God who takes sides and crushes enemies. The God of the New Testament is a God who reaches out to all men and women of every time and place. After Peter had been called to the house of Cornelius, the Roman centurion, he was able to say: "The truth I have now come to realise… is that God does not have favourites, but that anybody of any nationality who fears God and does what is right is acceptable to him" (Acts 10:34-35). Slowly but surely I believe we are coming to realise that very truth. I would suggest that our generation may be assisted by the extraordinary speed of progress in travel and communications that continues to make the concept of the global village a reality. But in the meantime we should not underestimate the battle that still has to be waged to root out the ingrained prejudices we may have against those from other ethnic and cultural backgrounds.

I think one of the joys of belonging to an international Congregation like the Redemptorists is that we have confrères on every continent. I have been privileged to attend our Moral Theology Congresses in, among other places, Santo Domingo, Thailand, Poland and Colombia. On those occasions we share the experiences of those living in wholly different circumstances, but the Gospel unites us in our search to bring hope no matter what the challenges or the scars left from the past. I will return to this theme when we come to try to unravel the meaning of salvation, but for now we will look a little more at what the Old Testament has to say to us about the nature of God.

A message that develops in understanding

We have already acknowledged that our own moral perceptions can develop and be refined and have noted a developing understanding of the nature of Christ's mission in the New Testament, even reflected in Christ's own understanding of what the Father was asking of him. It is not surprising, then, that we also see a real development in understanding through the Old Testament. The books written in the centuries immediately before the coming of Christ, and particularly the wisdom books, offer a very different image of God from those written in earlier times, though that is not an absolute rule. Even in the more ancient writings we sometimes see remarkable insights, particularly in the understanding of the prophets and the way they challenge the people. For example, the great prophet Isaiah begins his book by having God rebuke the people in this way:

What are your endless sacrifices to me?
says the Lord.
I am sick of holocausts of rams
and the fat of calves.
The blood of bulls and goats revolts me.
When you come to present yourselves before me,
who asked you to trample over my courts?
Bring me your worthless offerings no more,
the smoke of them fills me with disgust.
New Moons, Sabbaths, assemblies –
I cannot endure festival and solemnity.
Your New Moons and your pilgrimages
I hate with all my soul.
They lie heavy on me,
I am tired of bearing them.
When you stretch out your hands
I turn my eyes away.
You may multiply your prayers,
I shall not listen.
Your hands are covered with blood,
wash, make yourselves clean.

Take your wrong-doing out of my sight.
Cease to do evil.
Learn to do good,
search for justice,
help the oppressed,
be just to the orphan,
plead for the widow.

Come now, let us talk this over,
says the Lord.
Though your sins are like scarlet,
they shall be as white as snow;
though they are red as crimson,
they shall be like wool. (1:11-18)

Remember that Isaiah was called to be a prophet in around the year 740 BC. What a classic call this is to social justice. What more remarkable appeal could we ask for in terms of the integrity that being faithful to God requires? And of course you find this message repeated by the prophets over and over again as they make it clear to the people that there can be no room for hypocrisy. One of the most often quoted texts is from Micah:

What is good has been explained to you…
this is what the Lord asks of you:
only this, to act justly,
to love tenderly
and to walk humbly with your God. (6:8)

Jesus always challenged those who lived hypocritically. We see him continually facing down the Pharisees and their scribes, who would be meticulous in keeping all the prescriptions of the old Law, but many of whose lives were a contradiction. And of course Jesus questioned the point of bringing sacrifices to the altar should we be at variance with one another (Matthew 5:23-24).

The danger of proof-texting

When Jesus speaks we believe that we are hearing the definitive voice of God, and we will explore this idea shortly. However, when God speaks in the Old Testament we are caught in a conundrum. The prophets in particular speak for God and relay God's wishes to the people, but they are working in very different circumstances precisely because they preceded Christ and did not have the benefit of his revelation. The Old Testament authors express God's thoughts and actions in human terms. They had no other vehicle for communicating the message. It is not surprising that at times their anthropomorphism results in a distorted view of God. Understandably when the prophets are trying to bring home to the people the stupidity of their ways and the consequences of their behaviour, they will do it as graphically as possible and use human examples to reinforce the point. Of necessity theirs was a limited understanding of God, prior to the fullness of revelation that would come with Christ, and it is for us to make the necessary adjustments. If we are to grasp the message properly we should never lift passages out of context and we should always read individual books and passages in the light of the whole scriptural message. It is a great mistake to seize on a particular incident or saying and offer it as the definitive answer. This is known as proof-texting. When we want to make a point it is a great temptation and it can be done almost unwittingly.

I will give you an example from the work I did on the marriage question, which I wrote up in detail in my book. When asked about divorce, Jesus quotes Genesis and goes on to say, "So then, what God has united, man must not divide" (Mark 10:9). If we use this as the last word on the subject, as so many do, then we may conclude that there are simply no situations in which it is possible for Christians whose marriages have failed to be able to move on in life and form new relationships. However, we know that in fact the Church has struggled with this problem from the very beginning, and indeed the first recorded teaching in the New Testament comes in St Paul's first letter to the Corinthians, where he is dealing with newly converted Christians whose marriages have broken down precisely because they have become Christians and the non-believing partners have decided to leave. In these instances, although Paul urges them to try and make a go of it, if the non-believing partner insists on going, he advises that the Christian "is not tied". His reason: "God has called you to a life of peace" (7:15). So when trying to determine what God is saying to us in many of these delicate situations it is important to look at the whole scriptural message. Sadly, when doing my research on marriage breakdown, I found that even official church documents sometimes resort to proof-texting to make a point, but it does not make for sound theology.[2]

---

2 See T. Buckley, *What Binds Marriage? Roman Catholic Theology in Practice* (London: Continuum, 2002), p. 29.

Getting inside the message

I have explained the importance of looking for the connections and relating the word to our own experience, and we can do this with every part of scripture. This is not something that happens by chance but after we have made a serious effort to explore the meaning of the word before us.

For example, those of us called to preach will prepare for a particular liturgy by meditating on the texts and striving to understand what they mean for us. Bearing in mind that we believe that God inspired this word in the first place, it is good for us to pray for inspiration.[3] It is the Holy Spirit, who inspired the writing of the word, who also inspires us to understand it. Then we will need to situate the passages in their context and see what that teaches us about an author's train of thought. The books of the Bible are great works of literature and each section is put in a particular place for a particular reason. It is also important to be willing to look at biblical commentaries for information and facts we might not know. We cannot presume to know what the word means for us and our listeners if we do not take the time to try to find out what the person who wrote it meant and how the people who first read it understood it.

The book of Job

Of course some texts will take much more exploring than others, so may I suggest that one of the easiest ways of matching our experience with that of the biblical writers is to go to the wisdom books. There we will find a fund of wise counsel that has stood the test of time. The book of Job is a wisdom book: it is a wonderful story and will be familiar to many. It is a parable on the mystery of suffering that stands for all time. It describes the gamut of human emotions that erupt in the face of what seems like the injustice of it all, not to mention the complicated interplay of human responses to the one who is suffering. In the end the message comes through loud and clear: it is not within our compass to find an explanation. "The Lord gave, the Lord has taken back. Blessed

---

3   I am indebted to Jane Williams for the ideas I am sharing in this paragraph. At the Christian Resources Exhibition at Esher in 2007 she gave a wonderful seminar under the title, "Many words, one Word: igniting passion for the Gospels".

be the name of the Lord" (1:21). But ultimately the God in whom we put our trust is not an unjust God and justice will eventually prevail.

We do not have all the answers

As I look back over my life, over the history of the Judaeo-Christian community and indeed over the history of the whole world as far as I know it, I see so much that is beyond my understanding, but at the same time so much that catches my imagination and thrills me. When I am confronted by the kind of evil that I cannot understand I have learnt not to try to find an explanation or behave like Job's so-called friends. I have learnt that often I can do no more than stand alongside those who are in pain, just letting them know that I am there and that I care.

It was a lesson that took me time to learn. For a long time, and especially after I had been ordained a priest, I thought I would be expected to have something useful to say and I struggled to respond, often feeling hopelessly inadequate in the process. Indeed I well remember the occasion when I was confronted with the absurdity of my thinking and my expectations. Again I am indebted to my time at Creighton University in Omaha. It was during a course on spiritual direction that I was brought face to face with what had been going on for me. During a role-play session I was deputed to take the part of the director. The religious sister who was coming to me for direction had tipped me off that she would make life difficult by re-enacting an awkward situation she had encountered herself some time before. I was faced with a very disgruntled person who claimed that she should be with the poor people whom she had been looking after: she no longer believed much and certainly had no desire to pray and was there only because her superiors had insisted she come on retreat. I stayed calm and thought I had handled the situation well, gently leading her to the point where she at least agreed to go and spend some time with a scripture passage I was suggesting. I even managed to get her to break into a smile. We duly received the plaudits of the rest of the group and the sister assured me that she would have me as her spiritual director any time. However, the course supervisor was not so impressed. The giveaway line from me had been: "Will you just do this one thing for me…?" and the supervisor spent the remainder of the period trying to find out why I had been unwilling to stay with the pain – why I had kept trying to fix it. Of course she was right, and although initially I felt quite unnerved and even disturbed by the experience – the supervisor even came to see me in the evening to check that I was all right – gradually I came to realise that this was what I had been doing not just with the pain of others but also with my own pain all through my life.

As always the healthy solution is to be found in Jesus himself. It is a mistake to misinterpret the healing miracles. They were moments of grace and transformation in individual people's lives and often they touched the lives of others who witnessed them. Jesus was fulfilling what had been prophesied about him:

> The spirit of the Lord has been given to me,
> for he has anointed me.
> He has sent me to bring the good news to the poor,
> to proclaim liberty to captives
> and to the blind new sight,
> to set the downtrodden free,
> to proclaim the Lord's year of favour. (Luke 4:18-19)

This was what Jesus chose to read in the synagogue. When John the Baptist's disciples came enquiring whether he was the one they had been waiting for, Jesus sent back the same message:

> Go back and tell John what you have seen and heard: the blind see again, the lame walk, lepers are cleansed, and the deaf hear, the dead are raised to life, the Good News is proclaimed to the poor and happy is the man who does not lose faith in me. (Luke 7:22-23)

Those whose minds and hearts were open to Jesus were able to make the connections and experience the power of his healing ministry, but Jesus did not take away all suffering and death. Quite the contrary: those who were called to follow him closely were asked whether they could drink the chalice he was to drink (see Mark 10:38).

If we return to our meditation on !anguage we can find another way of pondering this mystery. The biblical revelation is really quite extraordinary: human beings search for words to describe God and their relationship with God, and then there comes a moment, which I would suggest is beyond even our imagination to have conceived – God chooses to come and speak to us in our own human language. "The Word was made flesh, he lived among us" (John 1:14). The Prologue of John's Gospel speaks to us of a Word that existed in the beginning, that was involved in the work of creation and that is the source of life and light. How do we understand this?

Here is one way I propose for meditating on the text: this Word of God was so powerful that it was actually God and then the Word was uttered for us and became one of us. Now we see the remarkable dignity that is ours, created, as Genesis tells us, in the image of God. The message now is that, in spite of everything, in Jesus we can and will be restored to our true dignity and identity. Paul works it out for us: we are brothers and sisters in Christ and therefore co-heirs to the kingdom of his Father (see Romans 8:14-17).

Chapter Eight
What does it mean to be saved?

Of all the chapters in this book this is the one on which I believe everything hinges. If you grasp the meaning of what I will share with you here you will understand the heart of Marty Palmer's scripture course and realise why my understanding of things was totally transformed by it.

Résumé

Firstly may I remind you of what we have said already about the revelation of God in the Old Testament. We have seen that God's chosen people recognised that they had been created by God and created for good, but that in their selfish desire to be in control they tried to grab for themselves the good things God had created. As a result disorder and disharmony ruled their relationships with God and with one another. Nevertheless they came to realise that God had not given up on them; and they waited for the fulfilment of the promise handed on through the generations from the time of Abraham that a saviour would come and redeem them. Their tortured and confused history is written up in the most wonderful literature: poetry and prose, parable and history, law and prophecy, prayer and thanksgiving. Even to this day they continue to wait for the one who will come and rescue their nation, which may begin to explain why the territorial battles in the Middle East remain so acute. When Jesus came two thousand years ago, he was not the type of saviour they had expected. While some recognised him as the one they had been awaiting, many missed the point. Their eyes were blind to what he was doing, their ears closed to what he was saying, their hearts hardened to his love and compassion.

Jesus could not force anyone to accept him or his message. That in itself would have been a contradiction of the message, which was that we had been created for love, which depends on freedom. So he had come to set us free, but people often chose to remain bound, especially by the shackles of their own sins.

The human solution

The human response to disorder in the world is to try to impose order. It is the only way we know and it is brilliantly described throughout the Old Testament, beginning with the descriptions of the potentates in Genesis and working its way right through to the Roman occupying army which held sway when Jesus came. It will always be difficult for us to grasp the utterly radical nature of Jesus' teaching because our experience tells us that the only way we can maintain a semblance of order in our world is through the use of, or at least the threat of, force. You only have to imagine the police going on strike for a few hours to imagine the probable chaos that would ensue, fallen human nature being what it is. Just think of the looting and general mayhem that follows a natural disaster when the normal controls are no longer in place. It is not surprising, then, that to a large extent the Old Testament view of salvation had concluded that it would be an exercise of God's power, forcing the rebellious into submission.

God's way

However, Jesus came with a message only of love. We had been created for love and the New Testament tells us that salvation is an act of God's love. The message is loud and clear: love is more powerful than force. Over and over again Jesus turns upside down our human way of doing things and appeals to us to look at the world in a different way. And in a sense he is always appealing to us to review our experience. We have seen that his kingdom is a kingdom of love and service where the last shall be first and those who lose their lives will save them. Our experience also tells us that the more we give, the more we receive in every kind of way. Again I use storytelling with the children to try to make the point, reminding them that if they are selfish with their sweets and their toys, it does not really make them happy. It is when they are generous and share and see how happy they can make others that they themselves become happy.

Jesus offers us the Beatitudes, a wholly new charter for living, which takes us way beyond the Ten Commandments. He calls us to unconditional forgiveness and shows us how to do it in his dealings with the disciples and all those whom he encounters, finally praying for those who crucify him: "Father, forgive them; they do not know what they are doing" (Luke 23:34).

When confronted by Pilate over whether he was a king, he did not deny it, but pointed out that his kingdom was not of this world (John 18:36). When the Pharisees asked Jesus when the kingdom of God was to come, he told them that it did not admit of observation so that one could say: "Look here! Look there! For, you must know, the kingdom of God is among you" (Luke 17:20-21). Previously, he had spoken of the kingdom of God having overtaken them, after their challenge about how he cast out devils (Luke 11:20). Jesus was establishing the kingdom in himself.

The problem for God's chosen people was that for the most part they were not ready for this wholly new and unexpected way of thinking and acting, albeit that it was all there in their scriptures. We have noted how meticulously Jesus' followers later pieced together the connections and in their scriptures (the New Testament) they are at pains to ensure that we get the message. Everything hinges on the resurrection. Without the resurrection nothing makes sense or fits together. With the resurrection we can make the connections and everything falls into place. St Paul could not have put it more powerfully or more simply: "If there is no resurrection of the dead, Christ himself cannot have been raised, and if Christ has not been raised then our preaching is useless and your believing it is useless" (1 Corinthians 15:13-14).

The saviour

The name Jesus means saviour. The words Christ and Messiah mean Anointed. The kings and prophets of the Old Testament were anointed and set apart for the service of God. The oil symbolised health and strength, and as we shall see it is one of the great sacramental symbols, setting us apart too for the service of God. Jesus Christ is the definitive one, anointed for God's purposes.

When we reached the key moment in Marty Palmer's course I will always remember him asking the class, which was about forty strong, this question: "If someone should stop you in the street and ask you if you are saved, what would you say? What do you understand salvation to mean? What is Jesus saving you from and for?" There was a sense in which all of us felt we knew the answer. We knew the old catechism, which stresses the fact that Jesus came to save us from our sins, but I think we all sensed that whatever anyone said, and quite a few volunteered answers, none of our answers would satisfy him. He pushed us further: "If I were to ask you to use your imagination," he said, "and picture yourselves not in a comfortable air-conditioned classroom in the middle of America, but in some seemingly God-forsaken corner of the earth, where with the local people you were experiencing real hardships and maybe even persecution, would your understanding of salvation still obtain?"

In fairness he was not trying particularly to draw us out on the issues surrounding liberation theology – he was pursuing an idea that was of immense importance and that would really help make all the connections. He insisted that any definition of salvation must fit every situation in which the Christian community might find itself.

Already he had got through to me – I could see how readily my priorities might change if my circumstances were radically altered or the course of my life had been different. By way of example today, I can picture myself in Zimbabwe, where I was invited a few years ago to give a retreat to our Redemptorist students. The London Province looks after a region centred on some townships on the outskirts of Harare. If that were my permanent mission I know that my prayer life and my preaching would be profoundly influenced by the very different circumstances from those in which I find myself in Britain.

So the question stands: what understanding of salvation will embrace any and every situation in every time and place? The answer that Palmer offered us staggered me in its simplicity. At the same time it transformed my whole understanding of the Gospel and the way I have lived and preached since. Firstly he took us back to that picture of the world painted in Genesis: a world wonderful in its beauty and potential, a world in which everything and everyone was created to be in harmony, but on which selfish human beings had tried to impose themselves. It remains a world broken and deeply divided, and we do not have to travel far to see those divisions and that brokenness. They are all around us; they are in every corner of the world.

It was into this world that Jesus was born two thousand years ago. He accepted our human condition and experienced the division and brokenness. However, he did not accept the division and brokenness. His whole mission was about healing and restoring us, and indeed the whole of creation. The miracles were not put on for show: they were Jesus' response to the broken minds and bodies that surrounded him. As we have noted, they were the fulfilment of what the prophets had foretold. St Paul and all the New Testament writers grasped this message in depth and always they are calling us to understand that *the work of salvation is the restoration of the unity and harmony that God had intended for us and the whole of the creation from the very beginning.*

This was the vision that Marty Palmer wanted us to see clearly. This was the vision that would make sense in every time and place. This was the vision that seized my imagination and suddenly put everything into perspective for me. I felt I had made a great discovery. I hesitate to use the comparison, but I felt my experience was akin to that of Thérèse of Lisieux when she was searching for her vocation and found in Paul's first letter to the Corinthians her answer. She realised that no one can be everything – apostle, martyr, prophet, doctor and so on – and at the same time that no vocation is of any value without love. She said that she cried out: "Jesus, my love! I've found my vocation, and my vocation is love." She went on to explain: "I had discovered where it is that I belong in the Church, the niche God has appointed for me. To be nothing else than love, deep down in the heart of Mother Church; that's to be everything at once – my dream wasn't a dream after all."[1]

My discovery was to see in the midst of the chaos of life a purpose. It began on the day Marty Palmer sent us off to read Paul's letter to the Colossians, with the instruction to note down as succinctly as possible (using no more than both sides of a sheet of paper) every reference we could find to unity and harmony. As soon as I began reading I was enthused by the challenge and the theme jumped off the pages at me. I have included my response to that exercise as an appendix to this chapter. From that day I have seen this call to unity continue to jump off virtually every page of the New Testament. Now I can see why everything that caused division and dissension caused Paul such distress. For example, there is a famous passage in his first letter to the Corinthians, where he pleads with them over their behaviour when they come together for the Eucharist:

> Now that I am on the subject of instructions, I cannot say that you have done well in holding meetings that do you more harm than good. In

---

1 Autobiography of St Thérèse of Lisieux, in *The Divine Office* (London: Collins, 1974), vol. III, p. 305*.

the first place, I hear that when you all come together as a community, there are separate factions among you, and I half believe it – since there must no doubt be separate groups among you, to distinguish those who are to be trusted. The point is, when you hold these meetings, it is not the Lord's Supper that you are eating, since when the time comes to eat, everyone is in such a hurry to start his own supper that one person goes hungry while another is getting drunk. Surely you have homes for eating and drinking in? Surely you have enough respect for the community of God not to make poor people embarrassed? What am I to say to you? Congratulate you? I cannot congratulate you on this. (11:17-22)

He goes on to remind them of the gift handed on to them and of how they should behave:

For this is what I received from the Lord, and in turn passed on to you: that on the same night that he was betrayed, the Lord Jesus took some bread, and thanked God for it and broke it, and he said, "This is my body, which is for you; do this as a memorial of me". In the same way he took the cup after supper, and said, "This cup is the new covenant in my blood. Whenever you drink it, do this as a memorial of me." Until the Lord comes, therefore, every time you eat this bread and drink this cup, you are proclaiming his death, and so anyone who eats the bread or drinks the cup of the Lord unworthily will be behaving unworthily towards the body and blood of the Lord. (11:23-27)

Above all, the Eucharist was to be a sign of unity. It was to unite them as the one body of Christ and yet there they were, not arriving in a fit state and proceeding to ignore one another and fail hopelessly in the call mutually to serve one another.

Paul repeatedly uses the image of the body to illustrate the call to unity. It always has a eucharistic overtone and is an immensely powerful symbol. Indeed it is in the next chapter of that first letter to the Corinthians that Paul explores in detail the analogy of the body:

Just as a human body, though it is made up of many parts, is a single unit because all these parts, though many, make one body, so it is with Christ. In the one Spirit we were all baptised, Jews as well as Greeks, slaves as well as citizens, and one Spirit was given to us all to drink.

Nor is the body to be identified with any one of its many parts. If the foot were to say, "I am not a hand and so I do not belong to the body", would that mean that it stopped being part of the body? ...

If one part is hurt, all parts are hurt with it. If one part is given special honour, all parts enjoy it.

Now you together are Christ's body; but each of you is a different part of it...
(12:12-15. 26-27)

In his Gospel John has his own way of inviting us to meditate on the mystery of our union with Christ and one another. In fact he devotes five chapters to the Last Supper. The description begins in chapter thirteen with Jesus demonstrating the kind of service he is calling for by washing the feet of his disciples. We have the image of the vine and the branches in chapter fifteen and then towards the end of the farewell discourses, as they are called, we are privileged to be able to listen in to Jesus praying. At the heart of the prayer is this petition: "May they all be one. Father, may they be one in us, as you are in me and I am in you, so that the world may believe it was you who sent me" (17:21).

Ecumenism

John XXIII, the remarkable Angelo Roncalli, who was elected pope at the age of seventy-six in 1958 and who turned the Church upside down by calling the Second Vatican Council, made that prayer of Jesus his own and so moved the Catholic Church towards ecumenical dialogue. Even as a youngster I remember rejoicing at this new spirit of goodwill and cooperation. I was fortunate that in the London of the 1950s and 1960s there was little bigotry, but I had learnt to be fearful of other Christian denominations and had been convinced any participation in their services would be sinful. Imagine my horror, then, when on a trip to town with my mother I noticed as we approached the doors of Westminster Abbey that there was a service in progress. I feared that her Anglican past might be about to take possession of her, but she turned away and said she would show me round another time!

At a stroke John XXIII had changed the atmosphere and towards the end of my time at school we were being sent on little missions to build up good relations with other churches in our neighbourhood. Once you grasp the call to unity as central to the New Testament message of salvation, nothing that helps to heal the wounds of the past is insignificant and certainly ecumenism can never again be seen as an optional extra. Nor can inter-faith relations and our dialogue with the whole of humanity.

Inner peace

As disciples we are called to be part of Christ's healing presence in the world, seeking every opportunity to mend the brokenness and bring people together. Eight hundred years ago St Francis of Assisi wrote his wonderful prayer:

> Lord, make me an instrument of your peace.
> Where there is hatred, let me sow love;
> where there is injury, pardon;
> where there is doubt, faith;
> where there is despair, hope;
> where there is darkness, light;
> and where there is sadness, joy.

Like all the great saints he was imbued with the Gospel and it was reflected in all he said and did.

This peace that Francis prays for is one of the great gifts the Lord offers us. We can go back to the Last Supper discourse to hear Jesus make this promise: "Peace I bequeath to you, my own peace I give you, a peace the world cannot give, this is my gift to you" (John 14:27). In Omaha in the summer of 1989 I was desperately searching for that peace and I was to make another great discovery, which was very personal. Still reeling from a sense of failure and brokenness after having had to leave the parish in Sunderland the previous Christmas, it suddenly dawned on me that this was not what Christ wanted. I was certain he wanted me to get it together, to be healed, to be at peace within myself, so that I could take up again my ministry in the life of the Church and bring that peace to others. This in itself would witness to the saving presence of the Lord, who continues to make all things new.

So there you have it: the more together you and I are, the more committed we are to seeking reconciliation with others, the more we reflect and take part in the saving work of Christ. The more you think along these lines, the more the truth of this message will strike you; the more easily you will see the unity and integrity of the Bible and the power of Christ's healing message. If this transforms your reading of the scriptures, be sure it will also transform your prayer and your understanding of the liturgy. At the heart of all the eucharistic prayers we see this invitation to be united in Christ, who offers us with himself to the Father. Therefore in a sense the whole of all the Catholic Church's eucharistic prayers is a call to unity, but I have taken the extracts below to show how explicit this call is.

Eucharistic Prayer I
We offer them [these gifts] for your holy catholic Church,
watch over it, Lord, and guide it;
grant it peace and unity throughout the world...
In union with the whole Church...

Eucharistic Prayer II
May all of us who share in the body and blood of Christ
be brought together in unity by the Holy Spirit...
May we praise you in union with them [the saints]...

Eucharistic Prayer III
Look with favour on your Church's offering,
and see the Victim whose death has reconciled us to yourself.
Grant that we, who are nourished by his body and blood,
may be filled with his Holy Spirit,
and become one body, one spirit in Christ...
Lord, may this sacrifice,
which has made our peace with you,
advance the peace and salvation of all the world.

Eucharistic Prayer IV
Lord, look upon this sacrifice which you have given to your Church;
and by your Holy Spirit, gather all who share this one bread and one cup
into the one body of Christ, a living sacrifice of praise.

Christ's abiding presence

As well as praying Paul's prayer from Ephesians at the beginning of conferences, I often remind myself and everyone present of Jesus' promises: "where two or three meet in my name, I shall be there with them" (Matthew 18:20) and "I am with you always; yes, to the end of time" (Matthew 28:20). We are not searching for a God who is at a distance, who is beyond the clouds, who has come and gone, doing what was necessary to save us and then leaving us to get on with it. We are celebrating a God who is close to us, living within us and the community. In recalling the memory of Christ's saving passion, death and resurrection in the Eucharist, we are not looking back nostalgically to what happened two thousand years ago but making those events present so that we might be part of them. "Do this as a memorial of me" (Luke 22:19). "I am the living bread which has come down from heaven. Anyone who eats this bread will live for ever" (John 6:51). It is the living God who has chosen to make his home with us (see John 14:23). Ours are lives to be lived to the full because we possess the Spirit of the living God, who was sent to lead us to the complete truth (see John 16:13). It is time, then, to think about prayer: that which unites us to the living God. In the next chapter we will look at liturgical prayer and in the following chapter we will consider personal prayer.

Appendix

My exercise on Colossians and salvation
(Scripture Course, Creighton University 1989)

Understanding "salvation" as being the restoration of our unity with God and each other through Christ, we can see the whole of Colossians as imbued with a concern for this unity and a warning against anything which could cause division. Further to this we can see that prior to coming to know Christ through baptism, people were effectively dead, but afterwards they become open to life.

The opening greeting declares that Paul is united with God – "Paul, appointed by God to be an apostle of Christ Jesus" (v. 1) – and that he and Timothy are <u>united</u> with the church in Colossae as brothers and sisters in Christ (v. 2). He reminds them that they express this unity by their "love in the Spirit" (v. 8)… "love towards all the saints" (v. 4); and clearly Paul is delighted to have received a report of their love through Epaphras. If they continue to live in this way they will "inherit the light" (v. 12). Their "hope is stored up in heaven" (v. 4), yet already they have a place in the kingdom of the Son (v. 13) and "freedom" and "forgiveness" (v. 14).

Paul explains how this happens in Jesus by linking their thoughts with creation and showing how Jesus is the first-born of all creation (v. 15) and "holds all things in <u>unity</u>" (v. 17), and how "all things are to be <u>reconciled</u> through him and for him" (v. 20). He goes on to point out that they are now reconciled by Jesus' death (v. 22).

Repeatedly he speaks of "hope": hope in the promises of Jesus (vv. 4, 23), "Christ among you, your hope of glory" (v. 27). So, as we shall see, there is more to be revealed.

At the beginning of chapter two Paul returns to the wider unity of the church: his struggles are all to <u>bind</u> them <u>together</u> in love, and that they may come to "full development" (v. 2). Again in verse 5 he is delighted to find them "all in <u>harmony</u>".

Now they are warned against those who might trap them with a "rational philosophy based on the principles of this world" (v. 8) and so deprive them of their freedom.

Then Paul comes to the heart of the message. They were <u>dead</u> because they were sinners (v. 13) but now through baptism they have been raised up with Christ (v. 12) and brought to <u>life</u> with him (v. 13).

The false teachers with their inflated opinions and worldly outlook are not united to the head. "<u>Jesus the head</u>" holds the whole body <u>together</u> and is the only way for us to reach full growth in God (vv. 16-19).

In the final paragraph of chapter two Paul asks them to check that they have really <u>died</u> with Christ to the principles of this world. He begins chapter three by confirming that now they have been brought back to <u>life</u> with Christ (v. 1), they can think about heaven (their hope). At present their life is hidden, but when Christ is revealed – and he is their <u>life</u> – they will be revealed in glory (v. 4).

Still there remains the danger of losing this life, so Paul now returns to the practical, and says "death" to all things which bring death. There is to be no evil or divisive behaviour; there are no distinctions now: "There is only Christ: he is everything and he is in everything" (v. 11).

Verses 12 to 17 are among the most often quoted, and beautifully express the things which make for this unity built on love. Paul prays that the peace of Christ may reign in their hearts because they were called together as parts of one body.

More practical advice follows on achieving this unity in the home. It will work if they all work for the Lord, who does not favour one person more than another (v. 24).

In chapter four, having promised his prayers for them, Paul, in turn, asks prayers for himself, and goes on to exchange and encourage an exchange of greetings. As in the rest of the letter this presupposes that their love for Christ is the mighty unifying force which makes sense of everything, even their sufferings.

Chapter Nine
Liturgical prayer

The Eucharist

We concluded the last chapter thinking about the Eucharist and I would like to spend some more time reflecting further on this mystery, which is at the heart of our lives as Christians. It is described in the Constitution on the Church of the Second Vatican Council (*Lumen Gentium*) as "the source and summit of the Christian life".[1] It is interesting that Pope Benedict XVI, by issuing in the summer of 2007 his Motu Proprio on the "Roman liturgy prior to the reform of 1970",[2] has fuelled something of a debate about the value of the reforms of Vatican II, but I would prefer not to get embroiled in that debate. In fact Pope Benedict explained that his purpose was to defuse the tension and resolve the divisions over the use of the former rite; and it should be clear by now that I applaud every effort that we make to heal the wounds of division and restore peace and harmony.

I was reared on the old rite and recognise that, especially when it was celebrated with solemnity, we were drawn by it into the mystery in a wonderful way. I can accept that we may have lost something of the mystique that surrounded such celebrations and it would be good if we could recapture the poetic beauty of a liturgy that helped us to stand together in awe before God. Certainly if we never give our young people liturgies that create a sense of mystique then I fear we are failing them, but, for all that, I rejoice in the reforms of Vatican II and the wonderful opportunities of renewal that they have afforded us. I believe the new rite too provides us with every opportunity to create beautiful and inspiring liturgies. It is always a temptation, no matter what the issue, to look back on the past through the proverbial rose-tinted spectacles and imagine that everything was so much better in a lost and bygone age. For all the beauty and splendour that could enhance the old rite I

---

1 Vatican II, Dogmatic Constitution on the Church (*Lumen Gentium*), 11.

2 Pope Benedict XVI, *Summorum Pontificum,* July 2007. A Motu Proprio is an apostolic letter issued by the pope and takes its name from the Latin, which means "on one's own initiative".

recall plenty of occasions when even as a child I was scandalised by the careless and slipshod way in which it was celebrated.

Then there is the criticism that the new rite does not place sufficient emphasis on the Mass as a sacrifice. I had been well instructed on the sacrificial nature of the Mass and I would not wish us to neglect that aspect today. In this mystery of faith, Christ's offering of himself on Calvary is made present for us, but so are the other key events of our salvation: his resurrection and ascension and of course the occasion of the institution of the Eucharist – the Last Supper.

Interestingly, before the radical reforms of Vatican II, I do recall a number of liturgical developments in the 1950s, most notably the restoration of the Easter Vigil, and there was also the introduction of what was called "the Dialogue Mass". When I was trained to serve Mass it was the altar server's prerogative to make the responses, but now everyone was being invited to make them. I cannot recall how many people were confident enough to try to get their tongues around the Latin and most of us still needed the vernacular translation at hand, even those of us who took Latin to A level! The indisputable fact is that in those days the Mass was often regarded as a private devotion and it is not surprising that many resorted to saying the rosary or other familiar prayers while the action went on at a distance. The rood screens in all our ancient cathedrals remind us of a time when the faithful were effectively cut off from the action altogether so that a server would have to ring bells to mark the time when the bread and wine were consecrated. Likewise the plethora of side altars reminds us of the many "private" Masses celebrated by the clergy, which again indicate that the Mass was often seen more as a private devotion than the assembly of the community.

Recovering the really ancient tradition

There is a wonderful reading on the celebration of the Eucharist from St Justin Martyr's *First Apology*, included in the Divine Office for the third Sunday of Eastertide, which is well worth quoting:

> On Sundays there is an assembly of all who live in towns or in the country, and the memoirs of the apostles or the writings of the prophets are read for as long as time allows.

Then the reading is brought to an end, and the president delivers an address in which he admonishes and encourages us to imitate in our own lives the beautiful lessons we have heard read.

Then we all stand up together and pray. When we have finished the prayer, as I have said, bread and wine and water are brought up; the president offers prayers and thanksgiving as best he can, and the people say "Amen" as an expression of their agreement. Then follows the distribution of the food over which the prayer of thanksgiving has been recited; all present receive some of it, and the deacons carry some to those who are absent.

Those who are well provided for, if they wish to do so, contribute what each thinks fit; this is collected and left with the president, so that he can help the orphans and the widows and the sick, and all who are in need for any other reason, such as prisoners and visitors from abroad; in short he provides for all who are in want.[3]

Here is a description of the Sunday Eucharist with which we can identify as we continue our efforts to implement the renewal envisaged by Vatican II. The priest is the president of the assembly and his task is to unite the community around the table of the Lord. During my years as a parish priest I was never in any doubt that the Eucharist was at the heart of the life of the parish. Erdington Abbey is a large parish with a small church and back in the 1980s we needed eight celebrations to manage the numbers who came. This meant that we were able to provide a variety of liturgies. There was a forty-strong choir which sang the more traditional music at a High Mass on Sunday morning and a competent folk group which sang at one of the evening Masses; there was also a family Mass which catered specially for the children. We did not have music at every Mass, but I like to think that at every celebration we made a real effort to engage the congregation and to celebrate with reverence and dignity. As president, much depends on the priest. He is not there to put on a performance, but he will have a considerable influence on the atmosphere that is created. If everyone is to be made to feel welcome, if those with particular gifts are to be encouraged to use them and if there is to be an atmosphere of prayer which recognises that we are all guests of the Lord, truly present in word and sacrament, it requires that the

---

3 St Justin Martyr, *First Apology,* in *The Divine Office Vol. II* (London: Collins, 1974), pp. 530-531.

president be sensitive, able to respond to the needs and the mood of the community gathered around him.

Teilhard de Chardin's "Mass on the World"

I can still remember the impact of a homily by one of my confrères during Mass on a school mission in Billingham in the north-east of England back in 1973. The circumstances were not ideal: the whole of what then was called the third year – that is, thirteen- and fourteen-year-olds – in the school hall on a miserable February afternoon. However, he held them spellbound. Using poetic licence he introduced them to Teilhard de Chardin, describing how this brilliant scientist – a palaeontologist – had travelled the world looking for fossils. After inviting the youngsters to recall moments when they had seen breathtaking views – maybe after reluctantly they had been dragged by their parents up a mountain while on holiday – he described how early one morning Teilhard climbed to the top of a mountain and looked out on the world as the sun was rising. He had us there on the mountain with Teilhard, stunned by the beauty of what lay before us and desperate to celebrate the wonder of it all. Pointing out that Teilhard was a priest as well as a scientist, he described how at that moment he was filled with a great desire to be perfectly united with God. He explained that, as a Christian, as a priest, Teilhard was moved to want to celebrate Mass: the perfect way of being united with God. But alas he had no Mass kit with him and so taking a pen and some paper he sat down and wrote instead. The result was his remarkable poem "The Mass on the World".

Moved by the beauty of the scene before him, Teilhard was also moved by what he could see only in his mind's eye. He took for his altar the whole of the world that lay before him. Then beyond the horizon he pictured the millions of people who would be rising from their beds that morning to go to work in the factories and the fields, the offices and the shops, the schools and the universities. At this point my confrère picked up the paten with the hosts and held it up before the young people. Onto the paten, he said, Teilhard placed all the work of the world. This was his bread and he offered it to God. Now it was time for the chalice to be held up dramatically before the congregation and we thought of Teilhard picturing all those who would not rise from their beds that morning because they were sick or suffering or dying. Their sufferings, their deaths were placed in the chalice. This was his wine and he offered it to God.

We went on to reflect that the mystery behind our taking the work of the world and the suffering of the world and offering them to God is that God not only accepts our gifts but transforms them and returns them to us as the gift of himself. When the priest stretches out his hands over the gifts of bread and wine and then utters the words of Jesus, "this is my body, this is my blood", the Spirit of God changes them into the presence of the Christ who had become our flesh and blood in Jesus. We went on to think about energy and light and fire; about God's Spirit reaching into all creation and into us at Mass; and about his coming as our spiritual food and drink, making sense of all our work and all our sufferings and even of death itself, which Jesus had overcome by his rising from death.

If the young people in Billingham struggled to understand the mystery they were not alone, for none of us fully understands – it is just that occasionally we get glimpses of the divine which lift us out of ourselves and remind us that one of the most joyful discoveries in life is simply that we can be full of wonder.

I like to think that in their school hall on that dark miserable afternoon the lives of those young people were lit up just a little and that they were in awe of the God whose Spirit reaches to the end of the earth and to every corner of the cosmos, the God who also held them in the palm of his hand and who wanted to feed them and make them whole. Certainly they remained amazingly attentive and their reverence when they received Holy Communion was remarkable. I too had been touched by the experience and I went home and read "The Mass on the World", something I would strongly encourage you to do, whether you are familiar with it or not.[4] Reading it again recently I realised that there were many connections I had not seen all those years ago, but which leapt at me now. Right at the heart of Teilhard's message is the cry: "Lord, make us *one*." There it was again, this message that I now see gives meaning to everything I believe and understand. Teilhard is not always easy to understand, but he draws us into a cosmic vision of God's saving presence, something we will explore a little more in the next chapter

---

4 "The Mass on the World" is chapter one in Teilhard de Chardin, *Hymn of the Universe* (London: Harper & Row, 1961). It can also be found at Religion-Online website: <http:// www.religion-online.org/showbook.asp?title=1621> accessed 16th February 2009.

when we look at private prayer. For now I will simply share with you how Teilhard leads up to that cry for unity:

> This bread, our toil, is of itself, I know, but an immense fragmentation; this wine, our pain, is no more, I know, than a draught that dissolves. Yet in the very depths of this formless mass you have implanted – and this I am sure of, for I sense it – a desire, irresistible, hallowing, which makes us cry out, believer and unbeliever alike:
> "Lord, make us *one*."

This is what every Mass is celebrating, whatever rite we are using, however many people are present, whatever the setting. It is the moment when heaven touches earth and the timeless God enters our time and unites us to himself and one another. It is vital therefore that always we go out of our way to bring this mystery alive for one another. It is not a private devotion. It is the community gathered in faithful remembrance and obedient to Christ's command: "Do this in memory of me." Our posture, our demeanour, the care with which we read and move, the use of candles and incense and music, all these things matter and make each Mass truly memorable.

Every Mass unites us with the praying Church all over the world, with everyone who has ever been present at Mass down through the ages, with the saints and the angels in heaven, because it unites us with Christ, the saviour of the world. In that sense there is only one Mass and it was offered at the passion, death and resurrection of Jesus. We are privileged that in every time and place those events are made present for us. We are partakers, not bystanders. Christ is made truly present in word and sacrament and we are privileged to be men and women of faith. And when our faith wavers, as it surely will, we can pray the words of the father who wanted his son cured, "Help the little faith I have!" or as the old translation put it: "Help my unbelief!" (Mark 9:24).

When you reflect on the wonder of the real presence, understand that while it is simply beyond our imagination to conceive of a God who literally puts himself into our hands, the gift is not there for us to hold back from and simply kneel before in awe, but for us to take and eat. We are being fed by Christ that we might live his life. We are temples of the Holy Spirit and if we recognise our own dignity as children of God we will surely recognise the dignity of our neighbours too. The point is that Christ is really present in the eucharistic species so that he might be really present in you and in me. With this in mind the penitential rite and sign of peace take on greater significance. We beg forgiveness of God – *and of one another* – so that nothing will spoil our coming together. We greet each other warmly at the sign of peace because we see in one another the presence of the Lord, who is about to feed us with himself.

The real presence and devotion to the Blessed Sacrament

Years ago I remember a speaker challenging those of us in the audience to explain our understanding of the real presence; and he tied us up in knots by asking whether Christ is really present when we listen to his word, when we celebrate the other sacraments, when we gather for forms of prayer other than the Eucharist, and so on. Many responded hesitantly and I recall him asking determinedly: Is Christ present or not? Are you saying he is more present at one time than at another? Can you divide up the presence of Christ into full and partial presences? It is important for us to be clear about this. Of course Christ is really present when we ask forgiveness for our sins at the beginning of Mass and listen to the scriptures in the liturgy of the word. What is special about the real presence in the sacred species is that they become the body and blood of Christ. The bread and wine themselves are transformed and do not have significance only when we receive them. We have read above how St Justin Martyr explained that the deacons would take the Eucharist to those who were absent; and it was that custom which led to reservation of the Blessed Sacrament and eventually to the great devotion that developed in the Middle Ages. It remains a wonderful gift to the Church and it is good to foster devotion to the Blessed Sacrament, for it is a powerful focus for our prayer. Whether during exposition or simply before the tabernacle, time spent in devotion to the Blessed Sacrament is a reminder that God keeps his promise and has indeed come to dwell among us and make his home with us. I recall once coming across a beautiful meditation that reminds us that we are more likely to recognise Christ in our neighbour in the midst of a garish and bustling world if we have spent time kneeling before him in the Blessed Sacrament: a salutary lesson worth remembering.

However, an important point to remember about devotion to the Blessed Sacrament is that it is never an end in itself. It is always linked to the celebration of the Eucharist and our participation in the saving mystery of Christ. St Alphonsus, whose own devotion was extraordinary, devised a way of achieving this link by making a "spiritual communion" when praying before the Blessed Sacrament: "My Jesus I believe that you are present in the most Holy Sacrament. I love you above all things and I desire to possess you within my soul. Since I cannot now receive you sacramentally, come at least spiritually into my heart. I embrace you as being already there and unite myself wholly to you. Never permit me to be separated from you."[5]

Sent forth

Just as our devotion is never an end in itself, so our celebration of Mass is not an end in itself. It is our participation in the saving mysteries of Christ – it is our participation in life and every aspect of life. It is called the Mass precisely because of the words the priest uses to send the congregation forth at the end. The Latin, "Ite Missa est", means "Go, the Mass is ended", and we have a number of formulas now, such as "Go in peace to love and serve the Lord", which make it absolutely clear that we are being sent forth with purpose: to be the light of Christ in the world, to proclaim the Good News, to heal the wounds of sin and division, to be a countersign to those who worship the false idols that arise out of greed and selfishness.

Looking for more connections

As you know by now I am keen that we continually look for connections and I think Teilhard's world view sees an interconnectedness throughout the whole of creation. If we pursue this idea a little we can see that just by drawing attention to him we are in a very real sense connected to Teilhard: to his ideas and also to him as a person. Then when we embrace the Christian vision of the communion of saints we are linked with him quite profoundly as a brother in Christ. I can illustrate this in

5 *Visits to the Most Blessed Sacrament and the Blessed Virgin Mary by Saint Alphonsus Liguori* (Missouri: Liguori Publications, 1977), p. 7.

a very concrete way. During a retreat in Dublin in the spring of 2003, I shared some thoughts about Teilhard with the Little Sisters of the Poor. To my delight one of the sisters came to me after the conference and asked whether I knew that Teilhard's own sister had been one of their sisters. I had not known this; but, thrilled with the connection, we talked about his wonderful spiritual insights. The following day she brought me a meditation of his, which I have used on retreats ever since. It is a wonderfully consoling message and invariably touches all those who hear it. The sister in question was not sure where it came from and to this day I have not been able to connect it with one of his published works. This is the meditation:

> Do not worry about the value of your life, its disorderliness, or the possible obscurity and gloom the future may have in store.
> You are doing what *God wants*.
> In the very heart of your worries and dissatisfactions, you are offering him the sacrifice of a heart that has been humbled and which, in spite of everything, inclines before an austere Providence…
> It matters little whether, in the depths of your being, you feel the heavy tendency to let yourself be weighed down by sadness at the sight of your failings.
> It matters little whether, humanly speaking, you feel you have "spoiled" your life when, as for God, he judges it successful and just as he would wish…
> Little by little, our Lord makes you his conquest and takes you to himself…
> Adore, and offer God your life which, to you, appears ruined by circumstances: what more beautiful homage than this loving renunciation of what one could have been!
> *Entrust yourself.*
> Blindly let go of yourself in trust: our Lord wants to make you worthy of himself and he will manage it, even if you remain in the dark up to the end, provided that you always hold onto his hand… and the more you are disappointed, the sadder you may feel, the tighter you should hold it.
> In a word, I tell you, be happy. Be at peace. Be untiringly gentle.
> Never let anything astonish you, neither your physical weariness, nor your moral failings.

Learn to have a smile always on your lips – a smile which reflects that of our Lord who wants to act through you and to "take over" all you do.

Above all else, in the depths of your being, place as the unchanging base of all activity (as the criterion of the value and the truth of the thoughts which fill your mind) the *peace of God*.

Whatever makes you tense or agitated is false; all the laws of life and the promises of God are there to prove it…

Since your action should have effects which are wide and long-lasting, it should spring from a heart which has suffered: this is the rule – a sweet and gentle one really…

Whenever you feel sad… adore and entrust yourself.

So Teilhard has given us the framework for our meditation on the Eucharist, which is the high point of all liturgical celebration. From it flows the whole prayer life of the Church, including all the other sacraments. In the Eucharist we pray over the gifts of bread and wine. Our prayer is that the Holy Spirit will overshadow them and transform them so that Christ may be present. There are echoes here of images at the beginning of Genesis of the Spirit of God hovering over creation and breathing life into us. It is this image that we can use in trying to understand all the sacraments. They are the signs of God's presence among us. Whenever we celebrate them we pray for the coming of the Spirit that Christ may be made present to heal us and forgive us, to strengthen us and protect us.

In most of the sacraments the symbolic laying on of hands to call down the Holy Spirit is quite explicit. We have seen that it is so as the priest lays his hands over the gifts at Mass. At confirmation, which is integrally linked with baptism, the bishop lays hands on the candidates. The laying on of hands is at the heart of the ordination ceremony and the anointing of the sick, and just as at confirmation it precedes the anointing with oil. During the sacrament of reconciliation the priest lays hands over the penitent during the prayer of absolution, something more easily done today when the barrier of a grille has largely disappeared and the priest is not reduced simply to holding his hand in the air. And although there is no explicit laying on of hands at the wedding ceremony, the bride and groom, who are the ministers of the sacrament to one another, do hold hands as they make their vows and the invocation of the Holy Spirit is certainly implicit in the ceremony.

I would go so far as to say that if we are to understand what is going on in all prayer, this is the starting point, and I will come back to it at the beginning of the next chapter, when we consider our personal prayer lives.

The Prayer of the Church

Before we move to the personal part of our prayer lives we will spend a while considering that other part of the liturgy, which is the Prayer of the Church, traditionally called the Divine Office. Again, it is one of the joys of the renewal since the Second Vatican Council that the Prayer of the Church has become more than just the preserve of monks and nuns in their monasteries and the clergy by virtue of their orders. The tradition goes back down through the centuries and emerged from the realisation that with the best will in the world it is not possible for us to be focused in prayer all the time and that according to the very nature of things we need to take time off to be with the Lord. Accordingly the monastic tradition developed with communities coming together many times each day and building their prayer lives around the recitation of the psalms. The Prayer of the Church is structured around Morning and Evening Prayer. The Office of Readings, Prayer during the Day and Night Prayer make up the whole, and in the stricter monasteries they would still assemble seven times a day for the different hours. What is heartening, however, is to note how many lay people have also begun to pray at least Morning and Evening Prayer and how many parishes include them on some days in their weekly timetables.

At a personal level I will always remember the struggle we had in the Redemptorist Congregation when the changes of Vatican II began to filter through. Many orders like ours did not have a tradition of praying the Divine Office in common. We met for our own morning and evening prayers, for periods of meditation in common, for an examination of conscience at lunchtime, and for night prayer before going to bed. Those who were ordained would pray the office privately and so fulfil their obligation. I can remember the concern among some of the older priests when we began to implement the recommendation that all religious communities build their common prayer life around the Prayer of the Church. One of the elderly priests who was teaching us scripture at the time protested that we were giving up beautifully crafted Christian prayers, including those of our founder, in favour of pre-Christian and at times very unchristian prayers. His argument seemed logical enough, but I must admit I have grown to value and even love the daily recitation of the psalms, whether as a community exercise or, when that is not possible, by myself. By way of an aside, it is well documented that St Alphonsus wished his Redemptorist priests and brothers to pray the Divine Office together, but somehow this was never enshrined in our rule of life until we implemented the reforms of the Second Vatican Council.

The psalms

There are a number of points that I think are worth making.

While it is true that with a few of the psalms we need to play mental gymnastics before offering them to the Lord, for the most part they are a wonderfully down-to-earth expression of every human being's concerns and provide us with a rich array of metaphors and images with which to speak to the Lord. At times the language is exquisite and a further reminder of the extraordinary literary treasure that is ours in the scriptures.

If I were to pinpoint a moment when I really began to appreciate this treasure, I would once again have to go back to that dark period in my life when I found myself languishing, stressed and depressed at the end of 1988. It was a matter of hanging on and somehow I carried on praying the Divine Office. Often it may have been perfunctory and just a matter of getting through out of a sense of obligation, but gradually I began to realise that these psalms were giving powerful expression to my deepest emotions, including my anger and frustration. It was almost as if they were giving me permission to tell God how I really felt. Just listen to this for a powerful way of expressing one's frustration to the Lord:

Lord, why do you reject me?
Why do you hide your face?

Wretched, close to death from my youth,
I have borne your trials; I am numb.

Your fury has swept down upon me;
your terrors have utterly destroyed me.

They surround me all the day like a flood,
they assail me all together.
Friend and neighbour you have taken away:
my one companion is darkness. (Psalm 87:15-19 [88:14-18])

When you feel a sense of injustice Psalm 7 provides some powerful words:

Lord, rise up in your anger,
rise against the fury of my foes. (v. 7)

When you cannot understand why justice and goodness do not prevail,
you might find some consolation in Psalm 9 (10):

Lord, why do you stand afar off
and hide yourself in times of distress? …

For the wicked man boasts of his heart's desires;
the covetous blasphemes and spurns the Lord…

His path is ever untroubled;
your judgment is far from his mind.
His enemies he regards with contempt.
He thinks: "Never shall I falter:
misfortune shall never be my lot." (vv. 1. 3. 5-6)

But of course the balance is always corrected and in the end you see that
goodness is destined to triumph. So the same psalm ends:

Lord, you hear the prayer of the poor;
you strengthen their hearts; you turn your ear
to protect the rights of the orphan and oppressed:
so that mortal man may strike terror no more. (vv. 17-18)

While a third of the psalms are lamentations, the book ends with some
of the most beautiful hymns in praise of God. Here is the final psalm in
the book, Psalm 150:

Alleluia!
Praise God in his holy place,
praise him in his mighty heavens.
Praise him for his powerful deeds,
praise his surpassing greatness.

O praise him with sound of trumpet,
praise him with lute and harp.
Praise him with timbrel and dance,
praise him with strings and pipes.

O praise him with resounding cymbals,
praise him with clashing of cymbals.
Let everything that lives and that breathes
give praise to the Lord. Alleluia!

Many mystics and spiritual writers have grasped these facts and written about them, so here is a flavour of what they have said.

Pope Pius X wrote an Apostolic Constitution on the Psalter in the Divine Office, part of which forms the second reading in the Divine Office on his feast day:

> From the beginning of the Church the divinely inspired psalms in the Bible have had a remarkable influence in deepening the devotion of the faithful as they offered to God a continual sacrifice of praise... Moreover... they have played a major part in the sacred liturgy itself and in the divine office...
>
> Saint Athanasius... goes on: "It seems to me that for him who recites them the psalms are like a mirror, in which a man may see himself and the movements of his heart and mind and then give voice to them."[6]

John Cassian, who lived in the fourth and fifth centuries, writes powerfully about the prayer life of the monk as follows:

---

6 Apostolic Constitution of Pope Pius X on the Psalter in the Divine Office, in *The Divine Office* (London: Collins, 1974), vol. III, pp. 207*-208*.

The living ardour of his soul will make him resemble, indeed, a spiritual deer, who feeds on the mountains of the prophets and the apostles, that is, who is filled with their most sublime and mysterious teachings. Vivified by this food on which he continually feeds, he is permeated to the point that all the sentiments composed in the psalms he recites henceforth seem, not as if they had been composed by the prophet, but as if he himself were their author, and as his personal prayer, in sentiments of the most profound compunction; at least he will think that they were composed expressly for him and he will know that what they express was not only realised long ago in the person of the prophet, but still finds its realisation in him every day. They no longer have the effect on us of having been memorised, but we bring them forth from the depth of our heart as sentiments that are natural to us and form part of our being; it is not reading that makes us penetrate the sense of words, but rather acquired experience… By this road our soul will arrive at the purity of prayer… This prayer is not taken up with the consideration of any image… no speech… no words… it springs up in… an insatiable impetuosity of spirit.[7]

For me probably the most compelling factor when it comes to praying the psalms is the fact that these were the prayers that Jesus used when praying to his Father. We know that he faithfully went to the synagogue with his disciples and we know that he knew the Hebrew scriptures through and through. And then we have those precious moments when we actually hear him praying the psalms – none more poignant than as he was dying on the cross and cried out the first words of Psalm 21 (22): "My God, my God, why have you deserted me?" (Matthew 27:46; Mark 15:34). When we pray through the whole of this psalm we see a kind of summary of Jesus' passion: Matthew and Mark clearly expect us to make the connection.

I have mentioned how not every Redemptorist welcomed the introduction of the Divine Office into the heart of our community prayer and I still hear some of my confrères and other priests bemoaning the fact that the psalms do nothing for them or complaining that the teaching Church even tries to dictate how we should pray, but I actually

---

7 Cassian's 10th Conference, in L. Bouyer, J. Leclercq and F. Vandenbroucke (eds), *A History of Christian Spirituality* (New York: The Seabury Press, 1982), vol. I, pp. 507-508.

believe they have missed the point. I hope I have made a sufficient case for the treasure that is ours in the psalms. But there is more: the Divine Office is not our personal prayer – it is the Prayer of the Church and we are invited to take our place each day among the communion of saints, singing the praises of God and pleading on behalf of ourselves and the whole of creation. Towards the end of the book of the Apocalypse there is painted in our minds a wonderful picture of Christ's final triumph and the feast that celebrates the wedding of the Lamb to us all. The voices of the crowd sound like thunder and everyone joins in the refrain of praise, "Alleluia!" (Apocalypse 19:1-10). This vision is bringing to a climax a theme that has run throughout the scriptures, which compares the kingdom to a great banquet, a mighty celebration, an uplifting liturgy.

Our liturgies here on earth are a foretaste of the great heavenly liturgy, but, more than that, our liturgies already unite us with the heavenly liturgy. I find it very consoling even when I am praying the Divine Office alone to think that I am united with millions of other people all over the world who are praying these same prayers: individuals, parish groups, little communities which may be struggling to keep going, large and flourishing monastic communities, the pope in Rome and so on. And then as the liturgical cycle unfolds we recall the saints who have gone before us and realise that we are linked in with them and the throng making up the heavenly host celebrating the heavenly liturgy.

We will come back to devotion to the saints and our Blessed Lady, but now it is time to move to the chapter that deals with the realm of our personal prayer life. It is unlikely that we will readily respond to the invitation to take our part in the great liturgical prayer of the Church if we do not also seek to develop and deepen our personal relationship with the Lord.

Chapter Ten
Personal prayer

Distractions

It would be impossible to estimate the number of times people have confessed to me, both inside and outside the sacrament of reconciliation, that they struggle with distractions at prayer. And of course I understand well what they mean because so do I. However, slowly I have come to the conclusion that much of the problem arises from a misunderstanding of what we are seeking and striving for in prayer. Again, I will be speaking from my own personal experience.

First prayers

I have already mentioned my gratitude for my parents and how it was with them that I first learnt to pray. Teachers and priests duly reinforced the notion that prayer was a time of communicating with God. The difficulty for young children is that while they quickly learn that human communication is a mixture of speaking and listening, it requires some growth towards spiritual maturity before we learn how to listen to God. And I suspect that this is not helped by the old hagiographies which often dwelt on the extraordinary visions of the saints and the apparitions to them, especially of our Lord and his mother. After all, we are trained to be suspicious of anyone else who claims to have seen visions or heard voices.

Not surprisingly, then, I think my formation in prayer concentrated almost exclusively on my efforts to talk to God. Even when I joined the Redemptorists and was introduced to St Alphonsus' method of mental prayer, which always begins with meditation, I did not really make the breakthrough, because the meditation was always regarded as a prelude to the actual prayer and I fear that I quickly concluded that true contemplation was beyond me: reserved for those called to the contemplative orders and a few other exceptional people.

The upshot of all this was that prayer became an exercise in concentration: a time when I sought to think about what I was saying to God. Couple this with those scruples I confessed to earlier in the book and you can no doubt recognise a less than healthy recipe for prayer and the spiritual life. Indeed when I was growing up I recall my tormented night prayers, which became a succession of extra "Hail Marys" for all the intentions that had come my way, from a sick aunt to the Cuban missile crisis. Add to this the concern that if I had not concentrated sufficiently on the "Hail Mary" in question it should be repeated, and you will have some idea as to why night prayers were not necessarily the highlight of my day.

Years later, as a young priest, I remember visiting a family where all the children were invited to pray spontaneously during a short prayer session before the youngest went to bed. I remember the panic as my turn approached. I was used to being asked to give a blessing but not to speaking from the heart, particularly after we had prayed for a poorly hamster and various other concerns that were close to the children's hearts. But it was wonderful and it was a lesson I have never forgotten. Likewise when Charismatic Renewal took Britain by storm in the 1970s, while it was not a movement that I found myself drawn to, I was grateful for what it taught me about freedom of expression in prayer, about that spontaneity which helps us to approach God honestly, like the psalmist.

Letting go

So, what I want to assert determinedly and confidently is that I have learnt that prayer is not an exercise in concentration. To begin with, the problem with such an approach to prayer is that it places the emphasis primarily on us and on what we are trying to achieve. We run the risk of seeing it almost as a performance for God, for which we might receive marks out of ten.

I now know for certain that prayer begins and ends with God. Indeed often it is not really necessary for me to do or say anything other than be present: "Here, Lord!" Prayer has much more to do with my openness to what is already going on, my seeing the connections, my getting in touch with God's Spirit, who is already within me. For me one of the most consoling passages in the New Testament is to be found in Paul's letter to the Romans. The context is fascinating because Paul precedes it by wrestling with what we might the call the great cosmic struggle. Just listen to how he expresses himself, culminating in that vivid comparison with a woman in childbirth:

I think that what we suffer in this life can never be compared to the glory, as yet unrevealed, which is waiting for us. The whole creation is eagerly waiting for God to reveal his sons. It was not for any fault on the part of creation that it was made unable to attain its purpose, it was made so by God; but creation still retains the hope of being freed, like us, from its slavery to decadence, to enjoy the same freedom and glory as the children of God. From the beginning till now the entire creation, as we know, has been groaning in one great act of giving birth; and not only creation, but all of us who possess the first-fruits of the Spirit, we too groan inwardly as we wait for our bodies to be set free. For we must be content to hope that we shall be saved – our salvation is not in sight, we should not have to be hoping for it if it were – but, as I say, we must hope to be saved since we are not saved yet – it is something we must wait for with patience. (8:18-25)

And then amazingly comes the contrast and its juxtaposition with his teaching on prayer:

The Spirit too comes to help us in our weakness. For when we cannot choose words in order to pray properly, the Spirit himself expresses our plea in a way that could never be put into words, and God who knows everything in our hearts knows perfectly well what he means, and that the pleas of the saints expressed by the Spirit are according to the mind of God. (8:26-27)

So there it is. The Spirit is already within us, expressing our prayer in a way that could never be put into words. When I set aside time for personal prayer, this is now my starting point: to be still and reflect on the mystery already unfolding within me.

Years ago I recall trying, when preaching, to reinforce this message with an illustration that appealed to me. As a child I was terrified of the water and although I loved the sea I did not learn to swim until I was in my teens. Eventually, one summer, I decided I would overcome my fear and make the breakthrough. I had often been assured that the water would hold me if only I would trust and let go, and that the best place to test this was in the sea where the salt water is more buoyant. I duly put it to the test and on a calm sunny day took myself to a quiet corner of the beach and in shallow water lay back and trusted. It worked and it was simply wonderful to find myself afloat. Thereafter I quickly learnt to swim. I compare prayer to this experience. So often we enter prayer struggling to stay afloat, fighting the water and the waves, when what is required is to lie back and rest trustingly in the arms of God. I will always remember that at the end of a mission during which I had shared this image, two middle-aged women came to me and announced that not only did they believe their prayer lives had improved, but they had also learnt to swim!

The prayer of breathing

In the summer of 1993 Father Bernard Häring came to England to give a retreat to his Redemptorist brothers. It was a moving occasion for all of us who were able to share it. Here was a man who had served the Church faithfully all his life: a theologian and a deeply spiritual man. I remember as a student having a great sense of pride when I learnt that he had given the retreat to Pope Paul VI and the papal household after the Second Vatican Council. Now here he was in his old age, speaking with an artificial voicebox after an operation for cancer of the throat, yet still faithfully proclaiming the Gospel.

One of the sessions that made a great impression on me was his instruction on the prayer of breathing. I believe it links seamlessly with all I have said above and offers a practical method of prayer that will be attractive and helpful for many.

He asked us to sit comfortably with both feet on the ground and holding a straight back. He recommended that we either close our eyes or focus on some object like a lighted candle or a crucifix. Then we were to become conscious of our breathing – the rhythm of inhaling and exhaling: the process that keeps us alive twenty-four hours a day, waking or sleeping. He told us to remain calm and composed and initially to do nothing more than be aware. He went on to invite us gently to take control of our breathing: without strain to breathe more deeply, gradually filling our lungs as we inhaled and fully emptying them as we breathed out.

At this point we were taken back to Genesis and reminded of the God who breathed life into creation. Immediately I thought of that wonderful hymn by Edwin Hatch:

Breathe on me, breath of God,
fill me with life anew,
that I may love what thou dost love,
and do what thou wouldst do.

Breathe on me, breath of God,
until my heart is pure:
until with thee I have one will
to do and to endure.

Breathe on me, breath of God,
till I am wholly thine,
until this earthly part of me
glows with thy fire divine.

Breathe on me, breath of God,
so shall I never die,
but live with thee the perfect life
of thine eternity.

Bernard Häring reminded us that all life is God's gift. As we breathed in we were to picture this breath of God reaching not just our lungs but every corner of our being, the top of our heads, the tips of our fingers and the tips of our toes. We were to become conscious of the Spirit flooding us with God's life. What better way can there be of bringing home to ourselves the Gospel message that we are temples of the Holy Spirit?

We were left for some minutes calmly entering into contemplation. But there was more. Having been reminded of the many obstacles that can arise, preventing us from experiencing God's presence – the cares and anxieties that dominate us, the habits of sin that weigh us down, the broken relationships that seem beyond repair, burdens that oppress us, leaving an empty void that we fear not even God can fill – we were reminded of Jesus' invitation:

Come to me, all you who labour and are overburdened, and I will give you rest. Shoulder my yoke and learn from me, for I am gentle and humble in heart, and you will find rest for your souls. Yes, my yoke is easy and my burden light. (Matthew 11:28-30)

Häring insisted that when we breathed out, we let go of all that was weighing us down. We were told to take Jesus at his word: "He will carry the burden with you; indeed he will carry it for you." I often think this is a message that we should shout from the housetops when we are talking about the sacrament of reconciliation. How often do people come humbly and honestly and confess their sins but somehow fail to lay down the burden? They leave the confessional room still carrying the weight on their shoulders instead of allowing the Lord to heal and transform them.

So there in a nutshell is the prayer of breathing. It is a simple and appealing formula. Many other religions practise similar forms of meditative prayer, which is heartening because it reminds us that there are common bonds that can form the basis of our interreligious dialogue. I remember once listening to a Thai bishop explaining Buddhist meditation techniques, but he was insistent that we take up the lotus position and endure the pain. For us as Christians it would be a way of uniting ourselves with the passion of Jesus. I must say that Häring's more gentle approach appeals to me. I think most of us would benefit more from defusing the tension in our lives than adding to it, but if a more demanding approach seems right for you, then follow the Spirit wherever the Spirit leads you.

Trinitarian prayer

When speaking of the sacraments we reflected on the fact that all our prayer is Trinitarian. The Trinity is not simply a mystery to be believed – it is our way of knowing God, indeed it is the way whereby we share in the life of God. It is the Spirit of God who breathes life into the Father's creation whereupon the Son, always present with the Father, can also be made present for us. There are some wonderful passages even in the Old Testament, which seem to foretell the revelation that will come with Jesus. In the wisdom literature in particular we see Wisdom compared both to the Spirit and to the Son of God:

> She is a breath of the power of God,
> pure emanation of the glory of the Almighty. (Wisdom 7:25)

With you is Wisdom, she who knows your works,
she who was present when you made the world. (Wisdom 9:9)

When he [the Lord] fixed the heavens firm, I was there…
when he laid down the foundations of the earth,
I was by his side, a master craftsman,
delighting him day after day,
ever at play in his presence,
at play everywhere in his world,
delighting to be with the sons of men. (Proverbs 8:27-31)

Then we see this mystery unfold marvellously at the annunciation, when Mary is assured that the Holy Spirit will overshadow her so that she might conceive and give birth to her son:

"The Holy Spirit will come upon you" the angel answered "and the power of the Most High will cover you with its shadow. And so the child will be holy and will be called Son of God." (Luke 1:35)

Whenever we pray this is exactly what happens again: the Spirit overshadows us, individually and as a community, so that Christ may be made present in us. And Christ in turn unites us and presents us to the Father. St Paul grasped this fact, realising that because of Christ's redeeming presence among us we become his adopted sisters and brothers, and children of the Father. We have the rights of children, becoming heirs to God's kingdom. If we can just begin to understand this message much of the picture becomes clearer and the jigsaw falls into place. Once we accept our dignity as children of God, breathing in and living the life of God, we see everything in a different light. We also see those around us in a different light, recognising that they too are called to that same dignity. At the same time, recognising our weakness and unworthiness, we become ready to make allowances for others and respond to Jesus' call not to judge or condemn. Stories like the Good Samaritan (Luke 10:29-37) and passages like the Last Judgement (Matthew 25:31-46) shape our thinking and our acting and we learn to reach out to others, seeing in them the presence of the Lord: "In so far as you did this to one of the least of these brothers [and sisters] of mine, you did it to me" (Matthew 25:40).

Accordingly we become more and more passionate about the questions of justice and peace in our world and spend ourselves in the service of all that breaks down the barriers caused by selfishness and greed. The Trinity is not an abstract concept that has nothing to do with all of this: it has everything to do with all of this.

On Trinity Sunday 2008 I did not have to look far for the subject of my homily. We had just had a remarkable demonstration of what the Christian life can look like when people open themselves to the power of the Spirit and allow themselves to be formed in Christ. An innocent young man, Jimmy Mizen, had been savagely murdered in Lee, south London, the day after his sixteenth birthday. Both his parents vowed that they would not allow bitterness to destroy them or the rest of their large family. They spoke only of forgiveness and their concern for the parents of the perpetrator of the crime. As Masses were celebrated in his school and parish it was clear that their faith meant everything to them. They grieved, but in the way Paul advised in his first letter to the Thessalonians: "not… like the other people who have no hope" (4:13). I was able to thank God for their witness and suggest to the congregation that here was a perfect model of what a Trinitarian prayer life looks like.

Prayer of petition

We come now to another key concept in prayer. In the New Testament prayer is always the prayer of petition and is distinct from thanksgiving. The time we spend seeking to enter into the mystery of God will lead inevitably to our pleading with the Lord for all that is still lacking in us and in our world. St Paul tells us to have the same mind as Christ Jesus:

> His state was divine,
> yet he did not cling
> to his equality with God
> but emptied himself
> to assume the condition of a slave,
> and became as men are. (Philippians 2:6-7)

When Jesus speaks about prayer he offers us some vital guidelines: "Ask, and it will be given to you; search, and you will find; knock, and the door will be opened to you" (Luke 11:9). The stories he tells are about people who will not be put off and he prefaces this teaching in Luke's Gospel with the story of the one who goes for some bread after his friend has gone to bed and locked up. The story ends: "if the man does not get up and give it him for friendship's sake, persistence will be enough to make him get up and give his friend all he wants" (Luke 11:8).

For sure God knows what we need: he will not give us a stone if we need bread or a snake instead of a fish (Luke 11:11). This of course gives us the clue. The prayer is not for God's benefit, it is for ours. Once we start asking we become caught up in the mystery of God and, dare I say, the more in tune we are with God, the more we realise that all our prayers are being answered because we begin to see beyond the immediate needs and crises. It is then that we are likely to see everything in the greater unfolding scheme of a God who is restoring all things in Christ, albeit amidst our pain and confusion. Here undoubtedly we are caught up in another of those great Christian paradoxes. We must offer petitions for all our needs: for those who are sick and despondent, for peace in every corner of the world and so on – and we must offer insistently – but what do we say to those who complain that their prayers are not answered? We can do no more than Jesus did and tell them to persevere, for in the persevering they may well find that their eyes are opened and they will see the bigger picture; and they may realise that their prayers have been answered, sometimes quite unexpectedly.

I can think of no better way of trying to illustrate this than asking those of you who are familiar with places like Lourdes to reflect on your experiences there. Millions of people flock to Lourdes every year, many of them with severe disabilities or illnesses. Occasionally we hear of remarkable physical healing, but very occasionally. At the same time I have never met anyone who has returned from Lourdes disappointed. Oh yes, sometimes people complain about the commercialism, but I am talking about those who are sick in mind or body and those who care for them. Somehow they always see the bigger picture in a place where those who are weak and vulnerable take pride of place, where the Gospel is lived as it were to the letter. Jesus never promises that all our troubles will be removed, but, as St Paul discovered, his grace is sufficient for us, his power is at its best in our weakness (2 Corinthians 12:9).

We return to that all-consuming fact of our faith that because of Jesus all our sufferings and our deaths now have real meaning: they are caught up in the passion and death of Jesus himself.

When you look back down the centuries you see how the saints and the mystics recognise this truth and latch onto it, and sometimes even in a mischievously humorous way. Famously, St Teresa of Avila, having been thrown from her horse into a mudbath, looked up to heaven and railed against the Lord: "If this is the way you treat your friends, no wonder you have so few of them." Since we have used the example of Lourdes we have only to think of the life of Bernadette Soubirous to see that, for all the extraordinary graces that have abounded as a result of her experiences in 1858, she herself was troubled throughout with poor health and a life of limited consolation. Indeed it would seem that the closer we get to the mystery of God's love, the more likely we are to have our share in the passion, but at the same time the more able we are to embrace it. Many bear witness to their share in what St John of the Cross describes as the "dark night of the soul". Only recently it has come to light that Mother Teresa of Calcutta admitted in her writings that for much of her life she experienced little or no consolation and had to depend almost entirely on the gifts of faith and hope.

If all this sounds a little depressing, it should not. Again we meet the paradox that in spite of the turmoil and the suffering there is a purpose and meaning to everything. Often it is only in the midst of the pain and suffering that we grow and become aware of the depth of untapped resources and strength within ourselves. We see more clearly the meaning of another of Paul's great paradoxes: it is when we are weak that we are strong (2 Corinthians 12:10).

The storm

There is another biblical image that I would wish to introduce here: it is that of the storm at sea (see Matthew 8:23-27). The story is one of those compelling moments in the Gospel when the disciples are astounded and you see their faith strengthened: "Even the winds and the sea obey him." As usual there is more to the story than meets the eye. The sea represented danger, darkness and the underworld for the people of the Old Testament. Jesus' action again confirms him as the saviour, the one who has power over the darkness.

Watch one of those remarkable television documentaries about the ocean and you realise that no matter how tumultuous the sea may be on the surface, when you go down into the depths you find a remarkable calm and beauty. If we transfer that image to ourselves, no matter what turmoil we may be facing on the surface of life, if we can find our way into the depths of our being (that inner room to which Jesus says we should go for prayer) we may find a peace and tranquillity that will enable us to cope. And indeed we can cultivate and more importantly pray for that peace. Jesus assured us that it was his special gift to us:

> Peace I bequeath to you,
> my own peace I give you,
> a peace the world cannot give, this is my gift to you. (John 14:27)

This is a gift that no one and nothing can take from you. It enables you to put everything into perspective, to recognise that Christ dispels the darkness and sheds his light on you and the world about you. In a sense this brings us full circle in our reflection on personal prayer. Always our prayer will lead us to the centre, the centre of our being and the heart of God. It is always the work of salvation, so it has to lead us back to the work of healing – healing and wholeness – oneness and unity for ourselves and the community as a whole.

Chapter Eleven
The intercession of Mary and the saints

Mediation

To complete our reflections on prayer it is important that we consider the importance of intercession. St Paul usually begins and ends his letters by calling for prayer and thanksgiving, often mentioning people by name. It is clear that we are interdependent in every aspect of life. You can illustrate this for children and young people by getting them to consider the complexity of modern living, beginning with how we get from A to B right down to how the milk arrives on the table at breakfast. This interdependence is never more obvious than when we are in need of care or nursing. That such care and concern should extend to and be embraced by our prayers seems to me to be the most obvious thing in the world.

It is interesting therefore that some Christian traditions struggle with any form of mediation other than that of Christ himself – and this largely seems to arise because of the statement in the first letter to Timothy that reads: "there is only one mediator between God and mankind, himself a man, Christ Jesus, who sacrificed himself as a ransom for them all" (2:5-6).

In the Catholic tradition this has never posed a problem. The unique mediation of Christ is precisely that he is the one who has redeemed us all and therefore restored the link between heaven and earth. Without Christ there could be no mediation, but, as we have seen, now we are all called to be the body of Christ. Because of his resurrection we are now able to live life to the full, but by the same token if one part of the body is in pain we all suffer. From the earliest days of the Church there has been a recognition that those who have lived close to Christ inherit the kingdom. Beginning with the martyrs from the early persecutions, those who have died in Christ have been held in veneration by the whole community. In death they do not cease to be our brothers and sisters. In fact quite the opposite: their prayers are considered to be even more efficacious.

Today saints are canonised by the Church only after a process of careful investigation into the sanctity of their lives, but this was not always the case. In the early Church they were canonised by public acclaim. In recent times we have seen something of a return to this kind of public acclaim in the way the faithful and even people in the wider world have reacted to the deaths of certain people like Mother Teresa of Calcutta and Pope John Paul II.

Of course the Church has always recognised that there are many saints whose lives never capture public attention – hence our celebration at the beginning of November of All Saints' Day and our commemoration the following day of All Souls. The latter is the prayer of the faithful on earth for those who need the Lord to make up whatever is still lacking in them before they can come to see the face of God. This wonderful tradition fills me with warmth and a sense of gratitude. It is another expression of that prayer of Christ that we may all be one – the message of salvation – the message that is at the heart of this book and that should help all of us to "take heart".

To summarise: when we ask for prayers from and for one another and when we invoke the intercession of the saints in heaven we are not interfering with the essential mediation of Christ in all prayer: we are simply doing what is most natural to us as humans, acknowledging that our lives are a constant interaction, which at its best involves goodwill and mutual care and support.

Seeking a good balance

I do not deny that it is possible for people to develop private devotions to Mary or certain saints that so dominate their spiritual lives that they lose a sense of proportion and can even lead them to superstition. The teaching Church recognises these dangers and always seeks to regulate such devotions by investigating their origins and offering guidance as to their authenticity. That said, I would wish to endorse the wonderful heritage that is ours and which encourages us to praise God for the gift of Mary and the saints, who are models of discipleship and whose care and concern for us enriches our prayer.

St Gerard Majella

Before concentrating on devotion to Mary, I will share some thoughts about one of our Redemptorist saints, Gerard Majella. In many ways Gerard's story is typical of so many of the saints, who appear as unlikely candidates for sainthood and who seem to achieve what they do against extraordinary odds. Born in 1726 at Muro Lucano in the mountains south of Naples, his route to becoming a Redemptorist brother was hardly straightforward. After a tough early life in which he earned his living as a tailor, supporting the family after the death of his father, he was rejected by the Capuchin Franciscans. Nothing if not determined, in his early twenties he pestered the Redemptorist missioners when they came to his town to the point where the mission superior sent him to the novice master with the now legendary testimonial: "I send you a useless lay brother."

Gerard duly completed his novitiate and in five extraordinary years developed an intense relationship with our Lord which bore fruit in his own life and in the lives of those around him. As with everyone and everything in the Christian life it was love that mattered. His love of God and of the people became the stuff of legends even in his own day and people sought him out for spiritual solace and support. How he became the unlikely patron saint of mothers and babies is also remarkable. When he dropped his handkerchief in the home of a family well known to him and one of the daughters picked it up, he told her to keep it as she might need it one day. Years later when she was pregnant and both she and the baby were in danger of death she remembered the handkerchief and asked Gerard to pray for her. She survived and duly gave birth to a healthy child. The story spread and so did devotion to Gerard as the mothers' saint. Tuberculosis ended Gerard's short life before he reached the age of thirty. He died in the Redemptorist community at Caposele, which also lies in the mountains south of Naples. Now the shrine of Materdomini there has become a shrine in honour of St Gerard too. It is a testimony to the fact that devotion to St Gerard shows no sign of diminishing that relatively recently a new viaduct was built across the mountains to accommodate the cars and coaches that make their way to this place.

When I was a novice and a young Redemptorist, Gerard never came across to me as a particularly appealing character. The hagiographers had dwelt so much on his levitations and other mystical experiences that he appeared very eccentric. However, I have grown to have a real affection for Gerard largely as a result of a visit in the 1990s to our house in Ciorani, a little village not far from Naples. It was to the Redemptorist community there that Gerard was dispatched by Alphonsus after he had been accused of sexual malpractice by a young woman who was in a disturbed state of mind after leaving a convent, which Gerard had recommended she enter. Faithful to the Redemptorist Rule that advised against defending oneself even against false accusations, Gerard suffered harsh treatment from Alphonsus and was even forbidden to receive Holy Communion. He was eventually exonerated when the accuser confessed that she had made up the story, but it seems that anyway nothing would have dissuaded the ordinary people from believing in Gerard. He had captured their hearts and their imaginations and his reputation was secure.

As I walked through the village with the rector of our monastery (wonderfully rebuilt after the earthquake ten years before) he, in between trying to goad the men to leave the bar and join us for prayer, confided in me that he had spent years trying to encourage devotion among the people to St Alphonsus. "It is no use," he said, "they have time only for St Gerard. They have never forgiven Alphonsus for the way he treated him." He spoke as if it had all happened yesterday and in an instant I felt a new sympathy for both these great saints. Their humanity shone through and I saw them struggling with an intense and delicate human dilemma, comparable to those that beset us in every generation and through which we too are called to be saints.

And there is more that leads me to see the interconnectedness of us all. St Gerard has always been the model for the brothers in the Redemptorist Congregation. Traditionally the brothers were very much cast in the role of servants to the fathers, but happily we have moved on since the reforms of the Second Vatican Council and I think have achieved a happier and less divisive community lifestyle. It is fascinating how often the quiet people in the background can have enormous influence. I am grateful for the dedication and good example of so many of the brothers from my earliest years in the Congregation and even before I joined. He will not thank me for mentioning him, but among us still is a brother whose total commitment is part of the folklore of our London Province. At the time of writing, Brother Malachy is in his early eighties and still continues to look after a substantial kitchen garden and provide vegetables and eggs for our pastoral centre in Scotland, not to mention his meticulous care of the church and sacristy. Of course life is never simply about what we do but who we are, and this man is gentle and prayerful and amazingly well read.

Brother Malachy was based in Bishop's Stortford before we left there in 1993 and it was there that unknowingly he had a major influence on a young man who had returned to England after travelling across the world seeking fame and fortune. The young man was fascinated by this quiet and unassuming brother whom he saw looking after the church and he wanted to know what made him tick. The rest is history. He joined the Redemptorists and is the only vocation among our brothers for a generation. He, Brother Michael, will not thank me for saying this, but he is a great gift to our province. During his time in training in Canterbury his pastoral experience was at the prison. He developed such a natural rapport with the prisoners that it was decided he should specialise in prison ministry, and subsequently he spent many years at Dartmoor before moving to work in a number of prisons in the north-east of England. He is a down-to-earth, sports-loving Lancastrian who relates to people easily and effectively. Like all our brothers he has got to know the story of St Gerard and developed a deep devotion to him. In fact his devotion is so infectious that it rubs off on the prisoners, one of whom painted a powerful new symbolic portrait of the saint to mark the centenary of his canonisation in 2004. Now this new portrait has spread across the world: I even saw copies of it when I was in Colombia for a moral theology congress.

Over and above all the extraordinary events that make up the lives of the saints and their occasionally miraculous interventions in the lives of others, it is this more ordinary interaction that for me enriches our understanding of the communion of saints and enhances our prayer lives accordingly.

Mary

It goes without saying that the greatest of all the saints is Mary, the mother of Jesus and therefore the Mother of God. From the earliest days of the Christian community Mary has held a place of special honour and it would be hard to find a canonised saint who did not have a deep devotion to her. It is not my intention to try to summarise all Mary's virtues and privileges: libraries have been written about them.

At the same time there is no doubt that Catholic devotion to Mary causes difficulties for some Christians from other traditions. I think this is unfortunate and would suggest that many of those difficulties are born of misunderstandings, some of which it may not be too difficult to dispel. Much of what we celebrate by way of Mary's privileges arises from what the Church concludes must have been so because of her unique role in the story of salvation history. Her "fiat" – let it be done according to God's will – opened the way for God to send his Son as saviour. There is a quite beautiful homily by St Bernard included in the Office of Readings leading up to Christmas, which has us waiting in suspense for Mary's response to the angel. Here is a flavour of what he writes:

> The angel is waiting for your answer... We too are waiting... Answer, O Virgin, answer the angel speedily... "And Mary said: Behold the handmaid of the Lord: be it done to me according to your word."[1]

So if you wonder about the virgin birth or the assumption do not be dismayed, just hear the voice of the community saying: "It must be so: God would surely have looked after this unique woman in a unique way." I think such a sentiment is best illustrated by meditating on the Immaculate Conception. It was defined as an article of faith only in 1854, four years before Bernadette had announced that this was the title with which Mary had identified herself – interestingly in Bernadette's own patois – at Lourdes. It is almost certain that Bernadette herself would not have been familiar with this title. Nevertheless for centuries Mary had been venerated under this title and the Redemptorists are proud of the fact that St Alphonsus had not only defended but championed this dogma in the face of serious theological opposition in his day. Sadly I fear there remains much misunderstanding about the meaning of this tenet of our faith even among Catholics. For a start, it has nothing to do with the conception of Christ or the virgin birth. It has to do with the conception of Mary in the womb of her own mother and it teaches us that from that moment she was preserved from the effects of the Fall, namely original sin. What it does not teach is that Mary did not need to be saved by the passion, death and resurrection of Jesus. Rather it was

---

1 St Bernard, Homily in Praise of the Virgin Mother, in *The Divine Office* (London: Collins, 1974), vol. I, pp. 141-142.

that those saving events of Jesus reached out to Mary from the moment of her conception rather than as they did for us at the time of our baptism. And this is not a matter of playing with words or concepts. If we fail to grasp this truth we run the risk of making Mary superhuman. She was not. Like her son she was totally human, living in the real world, above all living by faith. That is evident from the Gospel story. We see Mary questioning, anxious, wondering and pondering. We see misunderstandings, most notably after Jesus had got lost in the Temple and later when the family came to take him home because they thought he was going out of his mind.

Mary ponders

It is to Mary pondering that I would like to return and I am indebted for these ideas to Ronald Rolheiser and his insights, shared at a congress for the dioceses of Plymouth, Portsmouth and Clifton at Exeter University in the summer of 2004. He asked us to *ponder* on the word itself and asked what its opposite would be in the New Testament. He suggested, to our surprise, that the opposite is amazement, arguing that on many occasions the people were amazed at Jesus and what he was doing, when this was the last thing Jesus wanted. To illustrate the point we were asked to think of amazement as akin to an electric current. It can go through us and shake us up, but it does not lead to anything (dare I say as long as it is not too powerful!). He compared it to how we might react at a football match: we are amazed at the skill of one of the players in our team when he scores a brilliant goal. The problem is that shortly afterwards we may be stunned by the same player's ineptitude when he makes a mistake that leads to the opposition scoring. These experiences come and go, but they do not deeply affect us. So how is pondering to be contrasted to this?

St Luke tells us of Mary's pondering in the infancy narratives. We see her pondering after the shepherds' visit; we see her pondering after Simeon speaks about the child. The pondering goes on through her life and perhaps she never pondered more deeply than when she stood at the foot of the cross in silence. Notice she was standing, nobly, strongly. She was not collapsed in a heap; she was not screaming for someone to do something; she was quite simply present. And what was the nature of her pondering? She was not just thinking deeply about all that was happening and had happened: that is our Western definition of pondering. Rolheiser suggested that the Hebrew concept was more complex and significant, indicating that in some way Mary was participating in what was happening. His analogy for pondering of this kind was a water filter. Water filters are designed to receive water with all its contaminants and toxins and filter through pure, clean water. This, he suggested, was akin to what Mary was doing as she pondered. She stood alongside her son, filtering the sin and suffering of the world through herself so that pure love could flow from her. And this, he insisted, is the role of every true disciple.

You will realise why this image appealed to me, for, as I have already explained earlier in the book, I had to learn the painful lesson that often in my ministering I could do no more than stand alongside people in their pain and suffering, in their brokenness and disappointment. And here we were being invited to ponder the mystery that this was exactly what Mary did and that it was this that made her a true disciple of her son and united with him in his work of redeeming the world.

In the renewal that followed the Second Vatican Council great emphasis was placed on the importance of developing devotion to Mary that placed the focus on her faithfulness in responding to God's call and her example of true discipleship.

Our Mother of Perpetual Succour

One way in which I have tried to preach this as a Redemptorist is by using the icon of Our Mother of Perpetual Succour. (Forgive me for preferring the old English word, succour, to the now more commonly used word, help, because succour, as any dictionary explains, refers to help especially in time of need or distress. It also implies concern and involvement.) This ancient and fairly typical Eastern icon depicts Mary with the child Jesus in her arms. They are identified by the Greek initials for Mother of God and Jesus Christ. The archangels Michael and Gabriel carry the instruments of the passion and they too are identified by Greek initials. There is something enigmatic about the expressions on the faces of both Mary and Jesus. Mary is certainly looking out on us and it is often noted that from whichever angle you view the icon her eyes remain fixed on you. As a boy attending the Novena devotions in Clapham on a Saturday evening I heard many a sermon suggesting that

Mary was looking into our souls and reminding us of what our sins had done to her son.

There were also the sermons on Jesus, noting that he appeared to be looking up at the instruments of the passion and that this premonition of what he was to suffer so alarmed him that he shook with fear to the point where the sandal on his left foot is seen to be falling off. I would not wish to dismiss these interpretations out of hand, but I do believe there are other interpretations that offer richer and more biblically rooted insights into the meaning of the icon. In the first place it is important to remember that icons like this originated in an age when many people would have been illiterate and art was a key method of catechesis. There are lots of legends associated with the icon of Our Mother of Perpetual Succour, but we certainly know that it can be traced back for many centuries to the island of Crete and was brought to Rome by a merchant. It was venerated in the Augustinian church in Rome from around 1500 until the end of the eighteenth century when the Augustinians fled Napoleon's forces, taking the picture with them into the hills. When it was rediscovered later the following century it was given to the Redemptorists by Pope Pius IX for the simple reason that the Congregation had built its mother house and a church on the site of the former Augustinian monastery and tradition had it that this was where Mary had revealed that her picture was to be venerated, between the great basilicas of St John Lateran and St Mary Major.

As a catechetical tool the picture could be said to be summing up the heart of the Gospel story. It speaks to us of the incarnation: Jesus, the Son of God, is the Christ, the anointed one, who was born of the Virgin Mary. She in turn, by her "fiat", cooperated with God's loving plan and thereby shows us what it means to be a true disciple: one who listens to the word of God and keeps it (see Luke 11:28). This is the image of perfect love – of a God who loves the world so much that he sends his Son to redeem us, but the consequences of that love are his passion and death. Our call to discipleship will require that we understand this: that we are willing to take up our cross and follow him.

Understood in this way we see the instruments of the passion in the icon as being presented by the archangels to us rather than to Jesus – they are a reminder to us of the consequences of discipleship. I think there is a danger in making too much of Jesus having a vision of his passion as a tiny child in the arms of his mother. And it is this: that we do not grasp the depths of the mystery of the incarnation, the fact that Jesus was truly human. If we concentrate on the notion of the little child in the arms of his mother having a terrifying premonition of the passion, we may begin to think that he was not truly human – that in fact he knew everything even when he was a baby. We may forget that Jesus had to learn to walk and talk and mature in every way just like us. Remember how St Luke sums this up in his Gospel when Jesus returned with his parents to Nazareth after he was lost in the Temple: "Jesus increased in wisdom, in stature, and in favour with God and men" (2:52).

Furthermore I do not think the suggestion that Jesus was shaking with fear is the best explanation for the sandal falling off his foot. Better I think that we go to the book of Ruth and see what it says about the ancient custom of redeeming the land: "Now in former times it was the custom in Israel, in matters of redemption or exchange, to confirm the transaction by one of the parties removing his sandal and giving it to the other" (4:7). It may well be that the one who painted the icon knew his scriptures better than us and that this was just a further reminder that Jesus truly is the saviour of the world.

When Marty Palmer examined the human and divine knowledge of Jesus with us he accepted that we could never fully understand the mystery of the unity in one person of the two natures of God and man. But he said something that challenged me to ensure that my thinking was not verging on the heretical. He reminded me that Jesus was not a sort of hybrid, 50 per cent God and 50 per cent human: he was 100 per cent God and 100 per cent human. It is of immense importance that we grasp this fact while accepting our own limitations and ultimately our inability wholly to understand the mystery.

I think if we meditate on the icon of Our Mother of Perpetual Succour in the way I have suggested, we are more easily led to think about Mary's as a life of faith, pondering the mystery, while often herself not understanding.

Mary leads us to Jesus

Furthermore I do not think Mary looks out from the icon at us reproachfully. Rather she is presenting her son to us and calling us to discipleship. By the same token she is taking us to her son. And as I reflect on this aspect of the Christian mystery I see it to have been

Mary's role down through the centuries and celebrated all over the world today. What do the great shrines in honour of Our Lady do? They bring together God's people so that Mary can lead us to her son. We have mentioned Lourdes, which attracts hundreds of thousands of pilgrims each year, and there are other great shrines across Europe and across the world, including our own English shrine at Walsingham in Norfolk, which in recent times has become a wonderful centre of ecumenical activity. I had the privilege of visiting Aparecida, the national shrine to Our Lady in Brazil, in 2000. It attracts extraordinary crowds in excess of six million each year and the basilica holds 45,000 people. It is of special significance for the Redemptorists because our priests and brothers have been entrusted with the pastoral care of the pilgrims. And then there are the Novena devotions to Our Mother of Perpetual Succour. The inspiration of one of our American confrères in the 1940s, these devotions spread across the world and in some places, like the Philippines and Singapore, attract phenomenal crowds. When I visited Singapore in 2006 I was fascinated to see that the subway station near the Redemptorist church is actually called "Novena", and I witnessed the crowds who repeatedly fill the church from early each Saturday morning: estimated to be around 20,000.

Back in 1998 I was invited to be part of the preaching team at Clonard, the Redemptorist church on the Falls Road in Belfast, for the Nine Days of Prayer before the feast of Our Mother of Perpetual Succour in June. There 15,000 people pack the church and the corridors of the monastery at ten sessions each day. I was proud of my confrères there who have played such a significant role in the peace process in Northern Ireland, and I was honoured to share in such a powerful demonstration of faith. I took my lead from them, for their preaching was robust and uncompromising, calling for reconciliation in the Lord: the message to which we have returned over and over again in this book.

The rosary

No reflection on Mary would be complete without some thoughts on the rosary, this prayer that has sustained generations of Catholics and others for many centuries. Recently a friend of mine sent me a reflection on the rosary by the late Pope John Paul I. I have often wondered why the Lord let us have his smiling face as pope for only a month. He was obviously a very humble man, yet wonderfully gifted and well read. He was able to quote from the classical literature not just of his own country but of many others, including England. The book *Illustrissimi*, which was published in English posthumously, was a collection of letters he had written to famous characters while he was Patriarch of Venice.[2] Among those to whom he chose to write were Pinocchio, Dickens, Hippocrates, Figaro, Walter Scott and Charles Péguy. They provided clever and witty little sermons on a variety of questions. Here is what he wrote in a piece entitled "My Rosary":

> When people today speak of "adult Christians" in prayer, sometimes they exaggerate. Personally, when I speak alone with God and with Our Lady, more than as a grown-up, I prefer to feel myself a child. The mitre, the zucchetto and the ring all disappear. I send the grown-up on vacation and even the bishop, along with all the grave dignity and ponderousness due to his rank! And I abandon myself to the spontaneous tenderness that a child has for his mama and papa: to be – for half an hour at least – before God as I am in reality, with all my misery and with the best of myself. To let rise to the surface, from the depths of my being, the child I once was, who wants to laugh, to chatter, to love the Lord; and who sometimes feels the need to cry, so that he may be shown mercy – all this helps me to pray. The rosary, a simple and easy prayer, helps me to be a child again; and I am not ashamed of it at all.[3]

The family rosary

After the Rosary Crusade in the 1950s, like so many Catholic families across the country, ours attempted to be faithful to its daily recitation in the home. We did well for a long time, but at some stage, as my sister and I grew older and there were more and more occasions when someone was missing, it gradually fell into abeyance. Years later I recall my mother confiding in me that she had never found the rosary easy and I was relieved to know that it was not just me. Of course when I

---

2 A. Luciani, *Illustrissimi: The Letters of Pope John Paul I* (London: Collins, 1978).

3 See Catholic Pages website: < http://www.cin.org/docs/rosary-jpi.html> accessed 23rd February 2009.

joined the Redemptorists and was clothed in our habit I proudly learnt how to string the fifteen decades around the cincture (the belt that held the habit in place). Interestingly, to the best of my knowledge, no Redemptorist has yet added the five Mysteries of Light to his rosary: these were the extra decades introduced by Pope John Paul II.

For those who may struggle with the rosary I offer these few thoughts, which I hope will be of help. For some the rosary is a complicated prayer, calling for mental gymnastics. They struggle to work out how to meditate on a particular mystery while at the same time praying the "Our Father", the "Hail Marys" and the "Glory be". You will not be surprised to hear me say that I think it is best not to turn the rosary, any more than our other prayers, into a test of concentration. It may be that on occasion the words we recite become our focus and that is fine – let the mystery remain in the background on those occasions. Of course texts from the first two Joyful Mysteries, the Annunciation and the Visitation, form the first part of the "Hail Mary", so for those mysteries the two should come together. For the rest I think it better to try and focus on the mystery while using the most familiar of all our prayers to engage us as fully as possible. The very rhythm of their repetition can have a calming effect and when you think about it the prayer is designed that we may be totally occupied. Our minds focus on the great mysteries of salvation and therefore take us to the heart of the biblical message, while our bodies are occupied in reciting the prayers and fingering the beads, which ensures that the prayer is automatically timed.

When I still have difficulty with the rosary – and I do – I remind myself of all the great saints who persevered with it and used it to deepen their devotion to Mary. But more than that I think of the many people I have known who, especially at times of illness or approaching death, have remained faithful to this prayer – who would not be separated from their beads. It was as if literally they were clinging to this prayer, which had become so much part and parcel of their lives. They may not have been able to concentrate at all, but they could still work their way through the beads and know that with Mary they were in touch with God.

Holy Mary, Mother of God, pray for us sinners now and at the hour of our death.

Chapter Twelve
Reconciliation

I hope it has become abundantly clear by now that my intention in writing this book has been to encourage you to explore your own experience and in doing so to see the presence of God in your life, working to make you whole by healing any hurt or division. I believe that as this is true for you and me personally, it is true also for the whole of humanity and for the whole of creation. I believe too that the more we are in touch with this mystery the more we become that saving, healing presence of Christ in our own time and place. The world desperately needs peacemakers, those who go out of their way to seek reconciliation no matter how intractable the problem or hopeless the situation. The words of St Paul come to mind in this context: "My brothers [and sisters], never grow tired of doing what is right" (2 Thessalonians 3:13).

No matter how helpless you may feel, either about your own circumstances or about the wider world, no matter how powerless you may feel to be able to contribute in any practical way, never grow tired of praying for peace and reconciliation, and cling on to those beautiful words of St Paul's prayer: "Glory be to him whose power, working in us, can do infinitely more than we can ask or imagine" (Ephesians 3:20).

The sacrament of reconciliation

In the life of the Church we have the wonderful gift of the sacrament of reconciliation. Many non-Christian psychologists acknowledge that in this sacrament Catholics have a therapy of great value. The psychological advantages of being able safely to unburden ourselves to another are well documented and we will do well to reflect on this before we neglect this sacrament to the point of extinction.

That said, it is clear that the tradition of frequent private confession, which was part and parcel of my upbringing, has ceased to be the norm for the majority of Catholics today. As with most changes and developments of this kind the reasons are many and complex, and I will venture a few thoughts on the matter before sharing a reflection on the sacrament itself.

Changing practice

In my work on the breakdown of marriage I concluded that the teaching Church needs to review its pastoral practice with regard to those who are separated, divorced and remarried, and more than that review some of the theology that dictates the parameters within which we are able to work. My experience both as a penitent and as a confessor suggests that a similar honest reappraisal is called for with regard to the sacrament of reconciliation. I am baffled that a serious discussion on the question seems as far away as it was more than twenty years ago when I made little headway with one of our senior bishops, who told me not to be getting any clever ideas on the subject.

It may sound like a contradiction when I explain that the matter under discussion then was the number of confessions we faced especially at times like Christmas and Easter, and I was enquiring as to whether the experiment with general absolution, which had begun with such a fanfare and with seemingly such success in the 1970s, was simply to be consigned to history. The Vatican had reacted badly to the initiative of some of the English bishops at the time, arguing that the new provisions were exclusively for use in missionary countries where the ratio of priests to people rendered personal one-to-one confessions totally impossible. My contention was and still is that if as a confessor you are faced with long queues you become little more than an absolution machine and are unable to celebrate the sacrament with the care recommended: that is, by spending time reflecting on the word of God and praying with each penitent. I still find myself frustrated by the whole situation. It is not that I begrudge the time I spend as a confessor – far from it; I just believe we could do so much better and so much more. Let me explain.

It is true that for well over the last thousand years the custom of the private confession of sins, initiated by the Celtic monks, has been the norm. They had introduced the practice to contest the notion that this sacrament could be received only once after baptism and therefore was best left until near the end for fear of further transgression and a state of hopelessness. The monks rightly asserted that God was always ready to forgive and that Jesus had set the benchmark for us when responding to Peter's question, "Lord, how often must I forgive my brother if he wrongs me? As often as seven times?" by telling him, "Not seven… but seventy-seven times" (Matthew 18:21-22) – in other words, there is no limit.

Misunderstandings

As I found in studying the marriage question, the Church's instinct is always to find a pastoral solution to a pastoral problem, so we should have the courage to see new solutions to new problems. I would suggest that this is being faithful to the teaching of Jesus when he talked about not mixing new wine with old wineskins or patching an old cloak with unshrunken cloth (Matthew 9:16-17).

It seems to me that two elements of the story have become confused. It is clear that from the earliest days of the Church there was the realisation that if people offended in such a way that their sin became public and their situation a scandal, then they were debarred from the Eucharist and could only return to full communion after they had been reconciled with the community. In a later development, when moral theologians specified the gravity of certain actions or omissions, it was recognised that certain sins, even though they might not constitute a public scandal, could still be serious enough to separate us from the Lord and from the Eucharist. The title "mortal sin" is unfortunate, for nothing can kill the spirit within us or the soul, but it is reasonable for the Church to guide us as to what would be serious enough to deprive us of our place at the eucharistic table.

Sadly many among recent generations of Catholics were so haunted by the fear of mortal sin under the categories designated for them that they lost the ability to make mature conscience decisions. It is still not uncommon for older people to confess missing Mass on Sunday even though they were laid up in hospital and unable to move. When you try to reassure them, they respond by telling you that they would "rather be on the safe side"! So ingrained is this way of thinking that I have known people who would happily receive communion in hospital or at home but when well enough to return to church would not go to communion at Mass until they had confessed. Reluctantly I have come to the conclusion that it is better not to try to reason them out of their safety-first approach. I know that our Lord loves them in their confusion and I think deep down they know it themselves.

Suggestions

I am convinced that one way in which pastoral practice could be improved is if we made a clear distinction between a devotional use of the sacrament, and its celebration when people are conscious of grave sin that has ruptured their relationship with the Lord and his Church. The argument for devotional confession, as it used to be called, was primarily that it provided us with grace in the fight against sin. Again I would not wish to disturb the consciences of those who find this a helpful spiritual exercise, but, in view of the fact that fewer and fewer people are using the sacrament in this way, there may be a window of opportunity for us to think through the theology of the sacrament of reconciliation and reshape our pastoral practice.

On a recent retreat with the Portsmouth clergy, led by Timothy Radcliffe, we were reminded of the fundamental truth that in fact God has forgiven us from all eternity. What happens when we pray for forgiveness at the beginning of Mass or in the sacrament of reconciliation is that we celebrate that fact. Biblically we know this to be true. Stories like the Prodigal Son (Luke 15:11-32) readily give the lie to those who question this teaching. The Father is on the lookout for us and as soon as we turn back we are forgiven. And, more than that, this is also the way we are to behave towards one another. Indeed it is the only criterion we are given in the prayer Jesus himself gave us: "forgive us our trespasses, as we forgive those who trespass against us".

To encourage our congregations to think more about this might lead us to examine our consciences more maturely and might also lead us to a greater consciousness of the social nature of sin: the fact that sin is never just a personal matter, but affects the whole body of Christ – if one part is hurting, the whole body is hurting (1 Corinthians 12:26). My dream is that one day we will make more of this and in the first place really make use of the introductory rites at Mass. I occasionally suggest to a congregation that we imagine what it must have been like in the early days of the Church, when they met in one another's homes for the breaking of bread (see Acts 2:46). You can picture someone like Paul presiding and saying: "I hear that… there are separate factions among you, and I half believe it" (1 Corinthians 11:18), and then insisting that they sink their differences and forgive one another. Maybe this is the time when we ought sometimes to share the sign of peace?

Further to this subject, I know of one priest who gives general absolution during the penitential rite at funeral Masses, seeing it as a wonderful pastoral opportunity. Many priests would feel uneasy about taking the law into their own hands and it is a delicate area, for I accept that the Church is bigger than any individual. At the same time I think we also need to be willing to take the initiative and seize pastoral opportunities, for this in itself can be the catalyst that leads to change and growth in the wider Church.

My dream goes on to look forward to the day when we can have a series of reconciliation services during the year, especially in preparation for the great feasts of Christmas, Easter and Pentecost, and during them give general absolution. Our emphasis would be on encouraging everyone to grow in appreciation of the sacrament by spending time reflecting on the word of God, thereby deepening our sense of sorrow and our gratitude to God. At the same time we could highlight the value of personally confessing our sins when we are conscious of a grave problem or a habit of sin that may have taken possession of us, or when we know that a sin has separated us from God and the community. With such catechesis and practice I suggest our use of the sacrament would be more likely to have the efficacious value envisaged by the psychologists and lead to the change of heart called for by the Gospel.

Again I am grateful to Timothy Radcliffe for an example that captured my imagination and which I commend to those who fear we have lost our sense of sin. He described a bicycle journey on a freezing cold day, which rendered him so numb that on arriving at the front door of the house he was visiting he was unable to feel his fingers to press the doorbell and was reduced to using his elbow. He then described the excruciating pain once he got inside the house and the circulation returned to his fingers. I was able to identify with this immediately, remembering a number of similar occasions as a boy. He suggested that this might provide us with an insight into the pain of true sorrow as we expose the coldness of our hearts to the warmth of God's love. What a marvellous meditation that is: comforting and reassuring on the one hand; challenging and provocative on the other.

A service of reconciliation

I will conclude this chapter by sharing the format of a service of reconciliation that I have used in a variety of situations. With just minor adaptations, I have used it on retreats with clergy and laity, on parish missions, in the ordinary parish setting and in schools.

It was originally prepared by a group of students for whose pastoral training I was responsible and who worked with me for the whole academic year of 1994–95 in a parish in Ashford, Kent. During Lent we held a full-scale parish mission and each evening of the preached week different students took responsibility for working with parishioners in preparing the services. I must admit that I was like a cat on hot bricks for much of the time – so much for my faith in the students – and on the reconciliation evening I was certainly anxious that the format might be too ambitious. My fears were unfounded.

We had agreed that we wanted to keep the service simple and focus exclusively on the Gospel. I had reached a stage where I felt uncomfortable with the kind of service that was made up of long liturgies of the word, often including lengthy litanies and/or examinations of conscience on top of everything else. It was agreed that after a welcome and opening prayer we would focus on the story of the Samaritan woman in the fourth chapter of St John's Gospel. The students assembled a group of young people from the parish, some of whom read the different parts while the rest were to enact the story. As an exercise in good communication it worked beyond my wildest expectations. I sat in the front row and by the end there were tears in my eyes and I had to recover my composure before getting up to share some thoughts with the congregation. The most telling moment was certainly when the young girl playing the part of the Samaritan woman put down her water jar and went back to tell the townspeople what had happened. She strode purposefully from the sanctuary and down the centre aisle, really making eye contact with us and beckoning to us, in fact almost pleading with us, to return with her and meet Jesus. Whenever I have arranged a reconciliation service where we have been able to enact this Gospel story I have always stressed the impact of this moment in the story. It is another dream of mine that one day a congregation will become so engaged with the story that many will spontaneously get up and follow the girl back to the sanctuary. Meanwhile we make do with youngsters planted in the church, who step forth and make up the townspeople.

On this matter of becoming involved in the story, whether it is acted out or not, I always introduce the evening by explaining the simple format of the service and remind people that every story in the Gospel is personal to us. I encourage them to try to identify themselves with one or other of the characters or at the very least to be there as a bystander, intrigued by what is going on.

A wonderful illustration of how people become captivated by this biblical story was given to me by a foreign missionary. He described how he invited the people in one of his villages to discuss the story with him. "What time do you go to collect water from the well?" he asked them. "You know well enough, Father," they replied, "when it is cool, either first thing in the morning or last thing at night." "So what was this woman doing going out at midday – the sixth hour?" They had got the import of the story, for in chorus they replied that she may have been up to no good the previous night and therefore was too tired to get up early!

After the Gospel I draw attention to a few of what I think are the most compelling aspects of the story:

- In the first place there are only a few stories in the Gospel where we see someone banter with Jesus, and he obviously enjoys the exchange. Like the Syrophoenician woman, who talked about the dogs eating the children's scraps (Mark 7:24-30), this foreigner is more than ready to take Jesus on. He speaks to her of some mysterious life-giving water to which he has access – she responds by pointing out that she is a practical person and is at least armed with a bucket to collect her water. Ask yourself when you last bantered with Jesus in your prayers. It is surely good to aspire to that kind of confident relationship with the Lord.

- In the course of their encounter something happens that changes the mood and the intensity of their conversation. Jesus invites the woman to fetch her husband and she is forced to admit that that part of her life does not stand up to close scrutiny. You can well imagine that, when I was researching the breakdown of marriage, the fact that this woman had had five husbands was often raised with me. I scoured the biblical commentaries for a definitive answer, but none was forthcoming. Whether she had literally had five husbands or whether other explanations like the well being a place of courtship or the distinguishing religious traditions of the Samaritans give the clue, we will never know for certain. However, I think we can be sure of one thing: namely that something was seriously amiss in this woman's personal life. Furthermore, as a result of her conversation with Jesus, something dramatically changed and she began to see

139

things in a new light. In fact she was so excited that when she recounted the story she said that Jesus had told her everything she had ever done. I suggest this is a little of John's hyperbole, but the point is that this was the way it seemed to her. Jesus had put everything into a new perspective for her and she was so transformed that she became a disciple and wanted everyone else to be blessed in the same way.

- I think we can have no better image of what our encounter with the Lord in the sacrament of reconciliation should be like than this. I propose to the congregation that for an examination of conscience it will be sufficient for them to think only of those areas of their lives that they know in their heart of hearts need the light of Christ and the warmth of his love shed on them. After a time of reflection we make an act of sorrow together and then provide confessors for those who wish to confess. To emphasise the communitarian nature of the celebration I recommend that ideally this is not an occasion for spending time in counselling – if that is deemed useful or necessary both penitent and confessor are asked to see if an appointment can be arranged for another time. In this way the attention is wholly on the Lord and what he is doing for us both individually and as a community.

- There are one or two other refinements that I have found helpful. Firstly, I think it is good if the one presiding slowly offers the prayer leading to the words of absolution over the whole congregation so that the confessors simply need to complete the formula over each penitent. It is a beautiful prayer and may otherwise go unnoticed:

> God, the Father of mercies,
> through the death and resurrection of his Son
> has reconciled the world to himself
> and sent the Holy Spirit among us
> for the forgiveness of sins;
> through the ministry of the Church
> may God give you pardon and peace.

Secondly, during a recent clergy retreat the bishop stayed on the sanctuary to greet with the sign of peace all those who wished. As with everything this part of the liturgy was optional, but to the best of my knowledge everyone, whether he confessed or not, made his way to the sanctuary to be greeted by the bishop. I sensed that everyone appreciated the significance and value of the sign of peace in that context – it is something that every community could easily replicate with a chosen person to be that sign of unity.

The penance

If you can be confident that everyone will stay until the end of the ceremony, I think it is good to finish with a common penance and a final prayer and blessing.

The penance is not supposed to introduce a dampener on proceedings. It is our generous response to the Lord's love – a demonstration of our goodwill and our firm purpose of amendment. Over the years I have had some interesting experiences as a penitent. On one occasion I was asked what I thought I should do and, wanting to show willing, ended up doing something for a whole week. On another occasion I remember the confessor telling me to go and treat myself and celebrate the Lord's love and forgiveness. Recently I chose to share this anecdote at the end of a service in a parish, whereupon the parents of one family were cajoled by the children to go straight to McDonald's!

Usually I suggest that we pray thoughtfully through the "Our Father" – the prayer that Jesus taught us and the prayer that sums up all our prayers. I also ask everyone to conclude with "For thine is the kingdom, the power and the glory", remembering Bernard Häring's comment that he could not imagine Christians in the first centuries ending a prayer on the word "evil".

Chapter Thirteen
Living in hope

I hope that if you have come this far with me you have been heartened. There is much that could dishearten Christians in today's world, and I do not wish to underestimate or ignore that fact. However, I trust it is clear that my conviction is that Jesus will fulfil his promises and among those promises is the assurance that he will always be with us. This has to put every problem, every disappointment, every anxiety into perspective.

Identifying some of the problems

Nevertheless I do not wish to finish without acknowledging that there are a number of issues that face the Church in the Western world at this present time, which call for our prayerful attention and an honest response. From the heady days of the 1950s and 1960s when I was growing up and new Catholic churches and schools were springing up everywhere, we have arrived at a situation where we are trying to cope with a dramatic decline in the number of priests and, in general, a considerable decline in regular church attendance. I accept that certain factors have arisen to buck this trend, most notably the influx into Britain of Catholic immigrants from Eastern Europe and other parts of the world, but I would go so far as to say that the Church, as I knew it, is dying. I believe that we need to acknowledge this fact before we can begin to address the challenges that lie ahead. I also believe that we need to address the pain that this situation is causing before we can begin to address the challenges.

For example, as I have already noted, when I joined the Redemptorists in 1964 the Congregation had just built a new wing at the seminary to house sixty students. The numbers peaked at forty-nine and then rapidly declined. Today we have only two men under the age of forty and, while a few are showing some interest in our way of life, we have only one postulant and therefore no prospect of another ordination to the priesthood for many years. It is true that in other parts of the world some provinces are flourishing much as ours was forty years ago. Even in troubled Zimbabwe, the region attached to our province, we have a healthy number of young men in training, but nothing suggests to me that there is going to be a reversal of fortunes in the West, no matter how many vocation campaigns we run. I do not believe we have yet acknowledged, let alone addressed, the pain that this must inevitably be causing those of us who have committed ourselves to the priesthood and religious life, nor the knock-on effect of all this in the wider community of the Church. In recent times it has been a privilege and a pleasure for me to work with the clergy of the Portsmouth Diocese as they grapple with the practical consequences of a restructuring of the diocese from over ninety parishes to twenty-four pastoral areas. The project is ambitious and realistic, and is already beginning to serve the diocese well, but, as we tried to iron out some of the teething problems, I asked myself, and them, what should we do in ten years' time when even these radical rearrangements may no longer be practical?

Mission or maintenance

One of the great discussions in recent decades has concerned where the Church should be putting its energy. It is clear to me that if the Church is not missionary, it is simply not the Church. Jesus sent the disciples out to the four corners of the world: "Go, therefore, make disciples of all the nations; baptise them in the name of the Father and of the Son and of the Holy Spirit, and teach them to observe all the commands I gave you. And know that I am with you always; yes, to the end of time" (Matthew 28:19-20).

However, it has been widely felt by many in the West that, in spite of all the growth and development over the centuries, the Church had settled in the old Christian countries for maintaining its structures and systems and had largely lost its sense of mission. As Redemptorists we felt the challenge of this acutely as we preached our missions in parishes and schools up and down the country. Were we simply seeking out those who had strayed from the practice of their faith or were we also going out with a real sense of mission to those outside the flock? There was always the temptation to judge everything by the number of people who attended the special services, but even when the crowds came out we agonised over whether we were just preaching to the converted.

Today the debate is as robust as ever and our general and provincial councils continue to challenge us to reach out to those who remain "unchurched" (not the happiest of terms!). I welcome all the initiatives that continue to be taken in the field of evangelisation – it would be tragic if the younger confrères in particular lost their drive and apostolic spirit – but I can also sympathise with those who find themselves tired and dispirited.

Seeking solutions

Have you noticed that consultancy-speak today is all about providing solutions? I say this with great respect for my friends in this field, who were a great help to me during my time at Redemptorist Publications. There I enjoyed the challenge of pitting my wits against those in the business world; and often there were practical solutions when it came to improving our productivity and marketing and ensuring that we were following best practice with regard to management and personnel issues. Undoubtedly there are areas of church life that can benefit from this kind of robust analysis, but I fear that when it comes to most of the fundamental questions that present themselves there are no obvious blueprints we can follow.

Being a leaven

In spite of the success of projects like Alpha or processes like RCIA, I do not anticipate that we will see a wholesale conversion to Christianity from among those trapped in the lifestyles of our secular society or from among those who are deeply committed to other faiths like Islam. And I do not think we are selling out to maintenance over mission if we accept that in the first place Christians are called to be a leaven. The chosen people of the Old Testament came to this conclusion about themselves once they realised that God's care and concern could reach out to others. It is an image that Jesus himself uses for the kingdom: "The kingdom of heaven is like the yeast a woman took and mixed in with three measures of flour till it was leavened all through" (Matthew 13:33). Further to this, it is important to reflect on how the early Christian communities developed and maintained themselves. We could hardly accuse Paul of not having a missionary spirit, yet in his letters you also see his deep concern to maintain and strengthen the newly formed churches, ensuring that they did not become contaminated but rather remained an example to all around them.

Care in the community

As I grow older I am becoming more and more convinced that here in the West our first priority is to look after our brothers and sisters in the faith. If, in a desperate determination to be seen to be missionary and reach out to those outside the faith, we end up neglecting our own, what sort of witness can we possibly give to the wider world? "By this love you have for one another, everyone will know that you are my disciples" (John 13:35).

Keep talking

So what of the particular besetting problems that claim our attention and over which we may also feel fairly helpless? The changing face of society and the Church are inextricably linked and among the recurring questions for those of us in the Catholic Church are the following:

- What are we going to do when we run out of priests?
- Should celibacy be obligatory for the clergy?
- Should we at least reconsider the theology around the ordination of women?
- How can we educate the laity to take a full and active part in ministry and catechesis?
- How can we be a welcoming community when so many are officially excluded from receiving Holy Communion by virtue of their personal circumstances or marital status?
- How can we foster a fruitful dialogue with the authorities in Rome?
- How can we foster a fruitful dialogue with other Christians and other faiths?

And of course other Christian traditions struggle with their own lists. I watch in sadness and dismay the problems that have erupted in the Anglican Communion over the issues of homosexuality and the ordination of women to the priesthood and episcopate. As with all these matters, in our own traditions and in others, I think we must begin by praying fervently for dialogue in a true Christian spirit. When people resort to intemperate and condemnatory language it is hard to see how this can serve the Gospel call to unity.

Before attempting to respond to some of the issues above I wish to quote Ronald Rolheiser and Timothy Radcliffe again. At the congress in Exeter in 2004 I recall Rolheiser posing a similar list of questions and saying that as he travelled the world he was constantly being asked for the answers. He replied confidently: "The bad news is that I do not know the answers. The good news is that I know no one else who knows the answers. So my advice is: Do not give up on the meetings, for Mary and the apostles were at a meeting – a nine-day meeting after the Ascension – and it was then that the Holy Spirit came." When asked similar questions at the National Conference of Priests in 2002 Radcliffe was honest enough to admit that he too does not have all the answers, but he did suggest that it is a mistake to close the debate even on the more controversial theological questions. I am sure that both Rolheiser and Radcliffe are right. One of the findings of my research into the pastoral care of those suffering from the breakdown of marriage was that the Church's response had been constrained by the conflict that arises when you are convinced that you do have the answers, but those answers prove hopelessly inadequate to the situation that confronts you.

Absolutes

So much of our understanding in the Western tradition has been rooted in the conviction that the Church's theology is built on absolute principles, which faithfully reflect God's purposes and laws, and that they form a seamless and unbroken tradition of the truth. One of the problems with this is that there is a temptation to go far beyond the defined dogmas of faith and make almost everything an absolute principle. It is very difficult to have the kind of open and understanding conversation that Radcliffe calls for when you are confronted with a person who insists that everything is absolutely certain. Recently I was challenged in a debate during a clergy in-service training day by a quotation from a pope with the rider: "...and if the pope says so, that is good enough for me". Inevitably on such an occasion a murmur of approval will ring round the assembly from those who consider that the trump card has been played and there is nothing more to be said on the subject. Sadly this is respectful neither of popes nor of anyone else, and it does not do justice to the tradition of the Church. Certainly Paul would have been singularly unimpressed with the argument, bearing in mind that he fought Peter vehemently over the imposition of Jewish customs on the Gentile converts. And so it has been down through the centuries, as directives from popes have often been revised and reformulated in the light of new insights and new knowledge.

Vatican II and the hope it inspired

I am unashamedly a child of the Second Vatican Council. There are those who claim that the Council produced an unrealistically optimistic vision for both the Church and the world. Whatever one's judgement on that, there is no doubt that it consciously developed a theology of the people of God, which recognised that we are all called to the same holiness. We are also called to service, gathered in our local communities around the bishop, who, as a successor of the apostles, forms a collegial team with his brother bishops, among whom the pope, as Bishop of Rome and therefore successor of Peter, is head of the college and the centre of unity for us all.

Inevitably we have returned to the theme of unity. Unity, oneness, wholeness, integrity: it is the pursuit of these that helps me to see a purpose in everything. In calling the Second Vatican Council, Pope John XXIII met with much fear and opposition even among his closest advisers. He summed it all up during his wonderful opening address to the bishops:

> In the daily exercise of our pastoral office, we sometimes have to listen, much to our regret, to voices of persons who, though burning with zeal, are not endowed with too much sense of discretion or measure. In these modern times they can see nothing but prevarication and ruin. They say that our era, in comparison with past eras, is getting worse, and they behave as though they had learned nothing from history, which is, none the less, the teacher of life. They behave as though at the time of former Councils everything was a full triumph for the Christian idea and life and for proper, religious liberty.

We feel we must disagree with those prophets of gloom, who are always forecasting disaster, as though the end of the world were at hand.

In the present order of things, Divine Providence is leading us to a new order of human relations which, by men's own efforts and even beyond their very expectations are directed towards the fulfilment of God's superior and inscrutable designs. And everything, even human differences, leads to the great good of the Church.[1]

Is not this just a masterly piece of understatement? I find it truly consoling that John XXIII had no idea of what he was unleashing. It is well documented that he expected the Council to be over within months; and he was dead and buried long before it finished and the final hope-filled document had been promulgated.

The Church in the Modern World

Gaudium et Spes, the great Pastoral Constitution on the Church in the Modern World, begins:

The joys and the hopes, the grief and anguish of the people of our time, especially of those who are poor or afflicted, are the joys and hopes, the grief and anguish of the followers of Christ as well. Nothing that is genuinely human fails to find an echo in their hearts. For theirs is a community composed of people united in Christ and guided by the Holy Spirit in their pilgrimage towards the Father's kingdom, bearers of a message of salvation for all of humanity. That is why they cherish a feeling of deep solidarity with the human race and its history.[2]

When I first read *Gaudium et Spes* I was convinced that things could only get better and better. We were still on the crest of that wave in the mid 1960s when we presumed the Church would grow stronger and

---

1 Pope John XXIII, "Opening Speech to the Council", in Walter M. Abbott SJ (ed.), *The Documents of Vatican II*, translation ed. Very Revd Mgr Joseph Gallagher (London: Geoffrey Chapman, 1966), pp. 712-713.

2 A. Flannery (ed.), *Vatican Council II: The Basic Sixteen Documents* (New York: Costello; Dublin: Dominican Publications, 1996), p. 163.

stronger and when we believed that we had only to hang on in there and all the answers would emerge. In those days we were still familiar with the threefold description of the Church: Militant (on earth), Suffering (in purgatory) and Triumphant (in heaven). There was a feeling of triumph, almost as if the second coming was around the corner, but like those in apostolic times we have had to learn to temper our enthusiasm.

We know that much of the New Testament writing was intended to rally and encourage those infant communities to persevere when it began to dawn on them that Jesus' second coming might not be as imminent as they had originally anticipated. Facing at best the long, humdrum haul and at worst persecution, they needed encouragement to stay the course. In some ways we might see our own situation as comparable. After the euphoria of those heady days when I was a student and a young priest, I have had to settle down for the long haul.

Advent – the season of waiting and hope

I have come to love the Advent season. Of all the liturgical seasons I think it best encapsulates where we are in every generation during the Christian pilgrimage on earth. We are caught between the first and second comings of the Lord. We understand that already our salvation is secure – Christ has achieved it for us in his passion, death, resurrection and ascension. Eternal life is ours because the Spirit has come and continually makes Christ present among us, Christ now in glory. We believe that we have been made for glory and yet there is much that remains inglorious, so we live in patient hope for Christ's own return in glory to recapitulate everything and present it to his Father.

The Advent season is about waiting and there can be something very rewarding about the wait. Looking back on my childhood I realise that often, if not always, I enjoyed the anticipation of events more than the events themselves. When Christmas was approaching, I loved the build-up: learning the carols; visiting homes for those who were elderly or suffering from incurable diseases and putting on concerts for them; buying the cards and presents; putting up the decorations and looking in wonder at the presents around the tree, knowing that some would be mine on Christmas Day. Yet I also remember how often on the day itself people seemed almost too exhausted to enjoy the celebration. Somehow the presents, even those you had asked for, never quite lived up to expectation and there was that feeling of anticlimax which seems to be an inevitable part of the human experience on earth. Of course St Augustine summed this up, reflecting on his own experience when he uttered his famous prayer: "You have made us for yourself, and our hearts are restless until they rest in you."

Responding to the sadness

I began this chapter on what might have appeared a low note for someone who is claiming that his intention is to put fresh heart into his readers. I noted the depth of sadness many of us may feel as we see the demise of something that was not just familiar but that we cherished: namely the Church as we have known it.

Now it is time to deal with the demon inside that proposition and it is not an easy demon to slay. I think we need to apply a little lateral thinking.[3] When Marty Palmer was trying to help us understand the divine knowledge of Jesus, he asked two questions. The first was: "When did you know that you were a human being?" The second was: "When do you think Jesus knew he was God?" In responding to the problem I have just raised I am inclined to ask myself a similar kind of question, namely: "When did I accept that I am mortal – that I am destined to die?" I know that I have now accepted it and, while I am not presumptuous enough to claim that death holds no fears for me, I no longer live in dread of death as I did when I was younger. Christian psychologists will argue that we can only truly begin to live when we accept that we are going to die – it is another of those great paradoxes and of course it is what Jesus is saying when he says that those who lose their lives save them. The mystery of our salvation, of our redemption, is caught up in the mystery of death and resurrection. For men and women of faith, resurrection is all around us. Just listen to part of another of those second readings that we have in the Divine Office. This is Pope St Clement I writing to the Corinthians in the first century:

---

3 Lateral thinking is best defined as looking for solutions in unexpected places. It is based on the theory that we naturally think in well-defined categories and look vertically up and down those categories for the answers when in fact the answer may call for us to look sideways or laterally into other categories. Edward de Bono developed this concept in much of his writing.

Think, my dear friends, how the Lord offers us proof after proof that there is going to be a resurrection, of which he has made Jesus Christ the first-fruits by raising him from the dead. My friends, look how regularly there are processes of resurrection going on at this very moment. The day and the night show us an example of it; for night sinks to rest, and day arises; day passes away, and night comes again. Or take the fruits of the earth; how, and in what way, does a crop come into being? When the sower goes out and drops each seed into the ground, it falls to the earth shrivelled and bare, and decays; but presently the power of the Lord's providence raises it from decay, and from that single grain a host of others spring up and yield their fruit.[4]

It is when we see these connections in nature but above all when we experience them at a spiritual level that the truth of the resurrection takes possession of us and becomes a reality for us. It is then that we become truly liberated and further understand what Jesus means when he tells us that the truth will set us free (see John 8:32).

With that refreshing vision we no longer have to worry about the death of the Church as we have known it. St Alphonsus foretold that the Redemptorists would survive until the end of time, but while this may sound like a definitive teaching from a saintly man, it is not an article of faith. I hope Alphonsus is right, but we may find that in due course the Redemptorists have served their purpose in the Church and must give way to new and perhaps more relevant forms of community life that fit the needs of future generations. For now, those of us who are Redemptorists are called to remain faithful to our commitment and do all we can to build life-giving communities inside and outside our Congregation. The point I am making is that the Church as we know it may be dying, but there is an absolute in which I do believe absolutely: it is that Jesus will not abandon his Church or forsake his promises and his covenant with us. When two or three gather in his name, he will be there. One way or another he will be with us until the end of time.

---

4 Pope St Clement I, Letters, 24.1-5, in *The Divine Office* (London: Collins, 1974), vol. III, p. 694.

Living the new life of the resurrection now

The great insight that I received from the Second Vatican Council was that I am already living this new life of the resurrection. I believe this with all my heart and I rejoice in my brothers and sisters who during my life have witnessed to their faith in this mystery and have done it above all in the way they have approached their deaths. I am not pretending that every deathbed situation I have attended has been peaceful or consoling; some have been a real struggle for the people and for me. But I have also seen so many where faith and hope have triumphed and people have discovered that deep inner peace, which again is one of those special gifts that Christ promises us. I have seen it in my family, in the Redemptorists and in many friends and parishioners to whom I have had the privilege to minister.

And I am not speaking here only of people who have led long and fulfilled lives. I will never forget Kevin, a young lad of fifteen, who died of cystic fibrosis during my first term as a parish priest. I had got to know him well over the last two years of his life, but what was it that prompted me to visit him at ten o'clock on the night that he died? Certainly it was consoling for his parents and for me that he regained consciousness for just a few minutes and asked me to pray with him before falling back into my arms and dying. With that experience as with many others I can only look back in gratitude and thank God for the graces that come with them, albeit that I remain at a loss to explain why Kevin should have had to die so young. I remain equally at a loss to explain why providence does not always seem to prompt me to make the right decisions about when to visit or when to say the right thing. However, as the years pass, in the face of all those unanswered questions I find myself less and less disturbed and more and more trusting in God's power to restore all things in Christ.

A criterion for judging

Earlier in my reflections I dwelt at length on my conviction that salvation is clearly revealed in the New Testament as the restoring of all that is damaged and broken, so that we and the creation around us can be brought to fulfilment. I believe this provides us with the one criterion by which we can judge our own behaviour and that of those around us.

If what I think and what I do integrates me as a person, makes me whole and healthy, fills me with the inner peace that the Lord promised as his special gift, then I can know that what I think and what I do is of God and will bring me to fulfilment. Likewise, if what I think and what I do helps to heal the brokenness that I see around me and is concerned with restoring harmony and peace among others, then I can know that what I think and what I do is of God and is part of that process that is leading to the restoration of all things in Christ.

Broadening the vision

The wonder of all this takes us beyond a narrow and anxious vision that sees salvation as a tortuous struggle to keep in with God and scrape into heaven. I think it is good for us to broaden the horizons and let our imaginations run free. This is surely what St John was doing towards the end of his life when he wrote the book of the Apocalypse. It is not an easy book to interpret, but we need only think about the fantastic ideas that emerge when we dream to realise that John was drawing on the apocalyptic writings of old and matching them with the salvation promised by Christ. Again it is important to recall that he was writing for communities that for the most part were suffering persecution and were in danger of losing their first fervour or even giving up altogether. The overriding message, however, is that in the end Christ will triumph and there will be a great party, a wedding feast when the Lord will present us as a purified, spotless bride to his Father.

Salvation is not a lottery

For those of my generation and older our catechesis induced a deep-seated fear that we might miss out on the party. The dangers of rejecting the Lord's invitation were stressed and became very real to us and we worried about ending up with the door shut in our faces. But it cannot make sense to reduce our spiritual lives to a kind of lottery, akin to a game of snakes and ladders, with unsuspected pitfalls lurking at every turn. Bernard Häring dealt with this problem by developing a theology of the fundamental option: in other words, a theology that concentrates in the first place on what is the basic direction of our lives. If the basic direction is towards God and his invitation to unconditional love, then while we may fail to live up to our aspirations much of the time, our failures do not amount to a total rejection of God. There is no better way of meditating on this than thinking of how forgiving parents are of their wayward children. Of course it is possible for a rift to occur that does completely sever the relationship, but such experiences are rare. And if we want a consoling word from the Lord on the subject, we can find it even in the Old Testament:

> For the Lord consoles his people
> and takes pity on those who are afflicted.
> For Zion was saying, "The Lord has abandoned me,
> the Lord has forgotten me".
> Does a woman forget her baby at the breast,
> or fail to cherish the son of her womb?
> Yet even if these forget,
> I will never forget you. (Isaiah 49:13-15)

The more I minister as a priest, the more I stand back in admiration at how so many people cope when the odds seem stacked heavily against them. I find myself instinctively drawn to make allowances and be understanding when things go wrong for them. I am confident that this is a Gospel response, for Jesus did warn us not to judge. It is not that nothing matters or that we have gone soft in the Church today. It has more to do with trying to get the right perspective and getting a sense of proportion. I am baffled when I hear people say we are making things like confession too easy today. Why make things difficult? Do they not hear Jesus warning us not to lay unnecessary burdens on people? I am puzzled that at times the official, teaching Church in Rome seems to become preoccupied with what seem to me less important disciplinary matters within the family and even starts questioning the wisdom of the local bishops, when there remains so much to be done in combating the forces of evil and all around there is so much violence and distress.

Undoubtedly the work I have done among those who are divorced, separated and remarried has shaped my thinking. I still fail to understand why we are not doing everything in our power to reconcile and welcome back to full communion those who are trapped in seemingly impossible canonical situations when everything reasonable has been done to allow all those involved to move on in peace and justice. Here I am only echoing the words of Cardinal Basil Hume, speaking on behalf of the English and Welsh bishops when they made their *ad limina* visit to Rome in 1997.[5] As part of his formal address to John Paul II he said this:

> In this work of reconciliation we are continually confronted, as pastors, with the situation of those in an "irregular union" for whom there is no perceived possibility of canonical regularisation. We must maintain the clear and consistent teaching of the Church concerning marriage. We must also act pastorally toward those in this situation whether Catholics already or seeking full communion in the Church. In this century especially, the relationship between membership of the Church and reception of Holy Communion has been affirmed and appreciated. It is not surprising that, despite reassurances, those who are not permitted to receive Holy Communion find themselves estranged from the family of the Church gathered for the Mass. We are conscious of your deep concern for these couples and their families and your invitation "to help them experience the charity of Christ... to trust in God's mercy... and to find concrete ways of conversion and participation in the life of the community of the Church" (24th January 1997). We are anxious to receive encouragement from you to explore every possible avenue by which we may address this important and sensitive aspect of our pastoral ministry.[6]

More than ten years have passed and I fear we are no further forward on this matter. During our in-service clergy days in Birmingham, Archbishop Vincent Nichols (now in Westminster) drew my attention to the fact that Pope Benedict XVI, during a summer school on 25th July 2005, gave a compassionate response to a question raised on the matter by a priest of the Diocese of Aosta. However, by again insisting that these are highly complex problems needing further study, Benedict would only offer the reassurance that people in these difficult situations may still participate in the Eucharist and that by not receiving Holy

---

5 "Ad limina Apostolorum" is the title given to the official visits of bishops to Rome, when they pray at the tombs of the apostles Peter and Paul and have meetings with the successor of St Peter, the pope.

6 *Briefing* 27/11 (20th November 1997), p. 8.

Communion their participation touches into the Eucharist as the "sacrament of Christ's passion". I am left reflecting that something has to be radically wrong with our theology if we end up telling people that they are welcome to come to the banquet of the Eucharist but that they are not welcome to eat and drink with us. I was also disappointed to see him go on to reject the Orthodox solution "by economy" as seemingly unworthy of further reflection partly because further marriages are not sacraments but also, to quote him verbatim, because "the Eastern Churches… have conceded the possibility of divorce too lightly".[7] Both the Western and Eastern traditions have had a long struggle trying to find solutions to this most delicate and distressing of problems. As I will now try to explain I believe the underlying theology that governs the practice in the East at least demonstrates that there are deficiencies in our tradition, which require urgent attention. And I will always treasure Cardinal Hume making a quiet aside to me while I was doing my research: "Of course the East has the answer."

A fruitful ecumenical dialogue

I have spoken about some defining moments in my spiritual journey in this book and I wish to end with one that took place on 17th October 1995. It was a meeting with Archbishop Gregorios, the Greek Orthodox Archbishop of Thyateira and Great Britain, in his home in Paddington. It was the last piece in the jigsaw of my social research into the marriage question and we sat and discussed the meaning of *oikonomia* in the Orthodox tradition. He made me truly welcome and we explored together the pressure on all the Churches with regard to broken marriages.

After a while I realised that our conversation was a struggle because we were effectively talking completely different theological languages. It is true that the Orthodox find it easier than Catholics to move forward when a marriage has irretrievably broken down by using the principle of *oikonomia*, but they do not take it lightly any more than we do the complex legal process of annulment. It is just that because of *oikonomia* they are not trapped in trying to establish that the original marriage never really existed, when all the evidence points to the fact that it

---

7 Pope Benedict XVI, Address at Meeting with Diocesan Clergy of Aosta, 25th July 2005.

did, but that the couple sadly grew apart rather than together. In these situations they are able to stand back from trying to produce a theology that tidies the situation up and they stay with the sadness and the mess. They recognise that the bishop, the *oikonomos* (the one entrusted with keeping good order in the Church) has the authority to act on behalf of the Lord and enable people to move on in their lives in peace: the criterion Paul uses with the Corinthians over the matter (1 Corinthians 7:16). As with our tribunals the bishop is able to delegate this work to others, but the point I am making is that the Orthodox have a theology that accepts that often we cannot know the answers and can only move forward trusting in the mercy of God.

For me the moment of truth arrived when Archbishop Gregorios asked whether I could conceive of any situation that is beyond the saving presence of Jesus. Confronted with this question there was only one answer, and it is that profound belief that Jesus can reach into all our brokenness and redeem it that fills me with hope. I really believe that somehow it will work out: that Christ's saving passion, death, resurrection and ascension will consume all the evil and restore the whole of creation. This is not to underestimate the forces of evil or deny the reality of sin and the possibility of hell. However, it is to proclaim that I do not believe that the Lord died to save only a few chosen souls. I believe that we, Christ's followers, have been entrusted with the task of reaching out to our brothers and sisters with this message of salvation and that our only weapon is the love we have for one another. You cannot impose love; we cannot impose ourselves or our faith on others any more than Christ could when he walked through Palestine and Galilee. Like him we can only invite people to come and see.

Be gentle

Towards the end of his life Bernard Häring pleaded with John Paul II to be gentle with the Church. I am convinced that we need to be gentle with one another and be humble in acknowledging our mistakes and our failures. St Alphonsus often wrote to his confrères upbraiding them for their failure to keep the Redemptorist Rule and he warned them that he would be waiting for them at the gates of heaven. Redemptorists often muse that they are not so worried about meeting the Lord but are terrified of meeting Alphonsus. In my ministry I have come to the conclusion that I would rather the Lord accuse me of being too understanding than of being too hard. It seems to me that always the Gospel message comes down on the side of compassion and it is only those who harden their hearts, who do not accept that they are weak and need God's help, who have anything to fear.

Take heart

I want to remind you that I think it is good for us to be at peace with ourselves and one another. I believe the Lord wants us to be together in ourselves and united with one another and with him. I hope that your understanding of the Gospel leads you to be gentle with yourself and others. For those of us who tend towards perfectionism, there is a moment in Christ's teaching in the Sermon on the Mount which can be something of a nightmare. It is when he ends a sequence of teaching by saying: "You must therefore be perfect just as your heavenly Father is perfect" (Matthew 5:48). Before you despair and feel you can never make the grade, compare Matthew with Luke. At the end of the same sequence of teaching in the Sermon on the Plain, Jesus says: "Be compassionate as your Father is compassionate" (Luke 6:36). The teaching is the same. It is just that the perfection of the Gospel is not the perfection of the perfectionist but the compassion of the Lord. So take heart and seek to put fresh heart into others. Take every opportunity to heal the wounds of sin and division and you will not be far from the kingdom of God.

Expanding our vision

I have already mentioned how much I appreciated the opportunity to work with Bishop Crispian Hollis and the Portsmouth clergy in recent times and I have also enjoyed the opportunity to help with in-service training in the Birmingham and Menevia dioceses, as well as giving clergy retreats and days of recollection in other places. I hope that my experience in a wide field of ministry has enabled me to be sensitive to the particular challenges and pressures of clerical life today. In the aftermath of the horror of the clerical abuse scandals it is encouraging to see the wonderful level of trust that still exists between priests and people, and I would want to affirm the tremendous ministry of so many of my brother priests. I believe too that one of the great graces of the Church today is that we are all learning that it is not only priests who are called to minister but that there is a rich variety of ministries that can be shared by those who are not ordained and that in a very real sense the call of every Christian is to minister the love of God to others.

I have noted how the wonderful insights of Teilhard de Chardin can broaden our horizons and expand our vision of what God is doing for us: redeeming the whole of creation through Christ. In my ministry to priests, I have found them heartened and encouraged by a wonderful story about Teilhard during the last year of his life. Jean Houston, in her book *Godseed: The Journey of Christ*,[8] describes how a chance meeting with him in New York, when she was "a big overgrown girl" of fourteen led to a magnetic relationship, which transformed her life. In fact she all but knocked him off his feet as she rushed down the road, but when they met again a week later as she walked her dog through Central Park, they struck up a friendship which was to last until his death, meeting each week for walks through the park, although she had no idea of who he was until years later when she was studying theology and read his book *The Phenomenon of Man*. She says that "the walks were magical and full of delight" and that being with him "was like being in attendance at God's own party, a continuous celebration of life and its mysteries". Her mother was sceptical about her walking with an old man in the park so often, but she was moved when Jean assured her: "when I am with him, I leave my littleness behind". In today's world it is such a reassuring story of innocence and I pray that all of us, priests and people, will be able to recover the simplicity and goodness that it demonstrates.

Paul begins and ends his letters with words of encouragement, so we will give the last words to him.

> I want you to be happy, always happy in the Lord; I repeat, what I want is your happiness. Let your tolerance be evident to everyone: the Lord is very near. There is no need to worry; but if there is anything you need, pray for it, asking God for it with prayer and thanksgiving, and that peace of God, which is so much greater than we can understand, will guard your hearts and your thoughts, in Christ Jesus. Finally, brothers [and sisters], fill your minds with

8   Wheaton, Illinois: Quest Books, The Theosophical Publishing House, 1992.

everything that is true, everything that is noble, everything that is good and pure, everything that we love and honour, and everything that can be thought virtuous or worthy of praise. Keep doing all the things that you learnt from me and have been taught by me and have heard or seen that I do. Then the God of peace will be with you. (Philippians 4:4-9)

You are God's chosen race, his saints; he loves you, and you should be clothed in sincere compassion, in kindness and humility, gentleness and patience. Bear with one another; forgive each other as soon as a quarrel begins. The Lord has forgiven you; now you must do the same. Over all these clothes, to keep them together and complete them, put on love. And may the peace of Christ reign in your hearts, because it is for this that you were called together as parts of one body. Always be thankful.

Let the message of Christ, in all its richness, find a home with you. Teach each other, and advise each other, in all wisdom. With gratitude in your hearts sing psalms and hymns and inspired songs to God; and never say or do anything except in the name of the Lord Jesus, giving thanks to God the Father through him. (Colossians 3:12-17)

Be at peace among yourselves... Be happy at all times; pray constantly; and for all things give thanks to God, because this is what God expects you to do in Christ Jesus...

May the God of peace make you perfect and holy; and may you all be kept safe and blameless, spirit, soul and body, for the coming of our Lord Jesus Christ. God has called you and he will not fail you...

The grace of our Lord Jesus Christ be with you. (1 Thessalonians 5:14. 17-18. 23-24. 28)

Go forth in peace to love and serve the Lord...